BOOK of DREAMS

Gong Hee Fot Choy

BOOK of DREAMS

A Book of Numerology, Prophecy,
a Planetary Guide,
and the Chinese Horoscope

MARGARETE WARD

CELESTIALARTS
Berkeley • Toronto

Designer Brad Greene
Clip Art from Dover Publications

CELESTIALARTS

PO Box 7123
Berkeley, California 94707

or email us at www.tenspeed.com

Celestial Arts books are distributed in Canada by Ten Speed Canada,
in the United Kingdom and Europe by Airlift Books, in New Zealand
by Southern Publishers Group, in Australia by Simon & Schuster
Australia, in South Africa by Real Books, and in Singapore, Malaysia,
Hong Kong, and Thailand by Berkeley Books.

Library of Congress Catalog Number on file with the publisher
Printed in Canada

1 2 3 4 5 6 — 05 04 03 02 01

TABLE OF CONTENTS

Preface

Following the publication of my fortune-telling system, *Gong Hee Fot Choy*, many have requested that I publish a dream book. This dream book is my response to the public's demand.

What Is a Dream?

First I will tell you how to distinguish between a real dream and an unreal dream. Our soul is ever awake and guards our body both night and day. When the body sleeps the soul, like the wireless waves of the radio, travels many places and sometimes contacts other souls, and in this way dreams are made.

The unreal dream or nightmare, as some of us refer to a bad dream, is caused by the body cramping the heart, or you are lying in an uncomfortable position, or perhaps you have eaten something that disagreed with you. The soul takes the best care of the body, and when this condition exists, the soul knows the body's needs, and at once the soul will record a terrible happening to arouse the body so that it will change its position or wake up. You may dream that you are falling, or there is a terrible fire, or a bad animal is chasing you—something most generally to scare you—and when you awaken after such a dream, you will feel weak and exhausted. This is caused by the body not properly resting. This dream is called an unreal dream, so if you have such a dream, just disregard it, for it has no meaning whatsoever.

A real dream is one that takes place and does not disturb you, and you can easily recall every incident afterwards. It will seem very real. Dreams like this have decided meanings. They come as a forewarning of approaching good or evil.

To have the best guiding dreams you should go to sleep without worry. If you have troubles, relax—try to dismiss them from your mind. If you dismiss everything from your mind when you retire, your soul will record many happenings upon your blank receptive mind before you wake up. The soul goes here and there and contacts many places and other souls while the body sleeps, and the information the soul gathers while the body rests will help you solve your many problems in your waking hours, and a neutral mind will help the soul in receiving messages others send you from a distance.

In this book I have given you the psychic interpretation of nearly 600 dreams. The object of this dream book is to teach you to decipher your own dreams. It is very easy if you will quietly analyze everything you dreamed about.

The words I have selected to interpret for you are the most outstanding. Many words have a similar meaning and if I were to list all the meanings here, there would be much repetition. Many dreams, like words, have a similar meaning. I have given you thorough interpretations for you to follow in deciphering your dreams; for instance: Animals all come under the same classifications as far as interpreting their meaning. All flowers likewise have the same significance. All trees and shrubs indicate similar meanings.

Therefore, if I should list all of the different individual names of similar things it would merely make a repetition. When you are interpreting your dream, keep this thought in mind. If you cannot find the exact thing you dreamed about, try to find something listed in the book that is similar—something that falls into the

same category. Then quietly think of it and you will be surprised how you can interpret the meaning of your own dreams.

There are only three kinds of dreams—the actual contacts of your soul with others while you sleep, good prophecies, and warnings.

I hope this will teach you how to dream and how to interpret your dreams, and may all your dreams be helpful, guiding ones.

Margarete Ward

"And being warned of God in a dream, that they should not return to Herod, they departed into their own country another way."

Matthew ii, 12

A Message to You

FRIENDS: While demonstrating my fortune-telling game, *Gong Hee Fot Choy,* in stores throughout the country, I have met and talked to thousands of people. Many of them have brought me their personal problems and I can truthfully say that those who have followed my advice have been helped. I have shown them what can be done through the right thought. Each of us has his own problems, but no one has a problem which cannot be solved if he will tune in to the higher power and trust that he will receive guidance.

How can we tune in to this higher power? That is what most of us want to know. Everywhere we see people who observe religious forms, give to charity, etc., who yet do not receive the blessings that are rightfully theirs. Why is this? The answer is that they are not using foresight. They lament that if their foresight were as good as their hindsight they would be millionaires, yet they seem to make no effort to use or develop their latent powers or intuition. If they would heed the signs and warnings which are plainly given, instead of complaining of their lot and asking others to do for them the things they should do for themselves, they would achieve success and win the things they desire.

We are warned again and again by dreams and signs, but how many of us heed them? Read from the bible the story of the king's dream interpreted by Daniel (Daniel 2) or of Pharaoh's dreams interpreted by Joseph (Genesis 41). Now, if God warned people by dreams in those days, do you not think that He does so still? Yet how often do we hear one say, "So-and-so prophesied this accident," and "I had a feeling I should not do this, but I paid no attention to it," whereas, if he had heeded the warning he might have

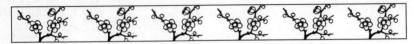

been saved disaster. We disregard these warnings, and when we must suffer the consequences we bemoan our fate. If we would only heed the inner voice, give thought to our dreams, and earnestly cultivate our foresight, we could not only avoid many troubles, but also achieve the success which we spend our energies in wishing for. And if the energy we expend in vain wishing, or in complaining, gossip, envy, and hate, were turned into constructive effort, how much we might accomplish, and how much sooner we should attain our goal, with plenty to use at our command.

We must listen to the inner voices, and we must put forth our best efforts, but we must also have patience. We become too anxious. We cannot wait. But the forces of nature are not hurried and we must attune our lives to the higher forces that govern the world. Listen to the words which Jesus spoke to a multitude of anxious men and women on a Galilean hillside:

> *Take no thought for our life, what ye shall eat, or what ye shall drink; nor yet for your body, what we shall put on. Is not the life more than meat, and the body more than raiment? Behold the fowls of the air; for they sow not, neither do they reap, nor gather into barns; yet your Heavenly Father feedeth them. Are ye not much better than they? Which of you by taking thought can add one cubit unto his stature? And why take ye thought for raiment? Consider the lilies of the field, how they grow; they toil not, neither do they spin: And yet I say unto you, That even Solomon in all his glory was not arrayed like one of these.*

Matthew 6:25–29

Many people pray for all sorts of things, and when their prayers are said, they forget what they have prayed for, or they sit down idly, hoping that their prayers will bring them what they want without any effort of their own, that fortune will fall into their

laps. What we must do is to decide what it is that we really want—setting our goal within reason and not expecting miracles—then listen to the voice within, seek guidance from the higher power, have patience and confidence, and put forth earnest and steadfast effort to achieve our desire. If we follow this rule, we shall perhaps not attain the goal we dreamed of, but we shall certainly come infinitely nearer to it than if we had spent our time merely wishing for it or seeking to attain it by lax, indifferent, or dishonest means. True, we will meet with reserves, but reserves are lessons given to develop our souls and make us strong characters. We should not beg in prayer for the things we want. No one loves a beggar who is not willing to work for what he gets; and who knows that the Higher Power does not become impatient with us when we whine and fret, like spoiled children, instead of putting forth our best efforts to help answer our own prayers? We should talk to the Higher Power as we would to a father, knowing that He knows what is best for us and will help us if we help ourselves. If we give our very best to every task, no matter now menial, using to the full all our God-given powers, and trusting our Father to know what is for our highest good, we may be sure that what is best for us will come to us in due time.

Never worry or lament over what is past.

Never indulge in self-pity; nothing can be more deadly to your growth.

Be thankful that you have been chosen to carry a burden, for this makes you strong.

Never envy another person his luck. Things do not happen by luck. We earn what we get—if not in one way, then in another.

Never wish that you had what belongs to another; wish that you had some like it. Do not envy another's wealth or success; be glad, as if he were one of your own. God has blessed him for something he has done, either in this life or the one just past.

Make friends with those who have plenty, for they can teach you how to get things to use for yourself. Remember that nothing in this world belongs to us; it is merely here for us to use. We brought nothing here with us and we can take nothing away. Those who seem to have more than we are merely using more than we are.

God has not made things in a small way. His blessings are unlimited. Therefore, we should never be stingy and saving for tomorrow, for who promised us tomorrow? Live today so that tomorrow you may say, "Yesterday, I lived." Tomorrow, if given, will be taken care of.

Don't worry; worry is a poison that destroys.

Remember that charity begins at home. Look out first for the needs of yourself and your own household. If all would do this, there would be little need for us to take care of others.

If someone is ill, help him; if someone is hungry, feed him; then try to teach him how to tune in to the higher forces so that he can care for himself in the future. Always seek to teach and help others, for there are many young souls here who need help.

When others are in sorrow or excited, remain calm. Know that whatever befalls them is for their own good. Even death is but a graduation to a higher plane of life.

Clean your mind of evil thoughts about others. If others repeat evil gossip, do not listen; forget it; don't repeat it.

Things are usually different from what they appear. Remember that there is a reason for everything.

If you hear that an unkind thing has been said about you, treat it like a mud puddle; step over it, not in it. Thus you will send the evil back to the sender and he will have it to cope with, for it did not belong to you in the first place.

Above all, think healthy thoughts, and when things do not turn out as you had planned, remember that the thing you wanted

was not meant for you and that there is something better in store for you.

If an enemy harms you by word or deed, wish him good luck and happiness with all the sincerity in your heart. Do not seek revenge. There are other forces which will mete out justice, and we need not bother. Leave your enemy alone with his thoughts, and his own thoughts will be his punishment.

Never say, "I can't do this," or "I can't do that." Try. You will find you can. The word *can't* has done a lot of harm in this world. The word *can* is the right word.

Since time has been set for our seasons, there is a time for everything. There is a time for work, a time for play; a time to sleep, a time to eat; everything has its rightful time. Since time plays so important a role in our lives, I am putting into this Dream Book the Planetary Hours for each day of the year, so that you can see the most favorable time for all your undertakings, such as buying, selling, calling, or anything you wish to do. Consult the Planetary Hour Guide before setting the time for doing anything that is important to you. Find the most favorable hour in which to do it. This Dream Book is different from others on the market. Its purpose is not merely to interpret your dreams, but to teach you how to unfold the meaning of your own dreams so that you may use them to guide you. It would be impossible to print here every dream, but they have been so classified that the reader may quickly learn how to interpret his own dreams.

No matter how bad your dream may be, if there is some good part in it somewhere, the good part modifies or lessens the bad. On the other hand, if a good dream contains a little bad, you may be sure that the better part will prevail; things will change for the better.

I do hope that some day people will stop, look, and listen to their small, still voice that is always trying to speak to them. When they

do, they will receive continual spiritual help. We are all born prophets, but we do not use our gift. We are too busy with worldly affairs to see the spiritual realm surrounding us. Why? Just because we can see the material things and cannot see the spiritual. We want proof to manifest itself in worldly possessions, and we want miracles to happen. We do not want to wait for the higher forces to give us, in due course, the things we should have. Oh, impatient people! How I would like to shake you when I see you take life so seriously, your faces all wrinkled with worry. The higher forces love you as well as anyone else. Give them a chance to help you. Send out thoughts of love to everyone. Smile; it costs you nothing.

In the hurry of life, we forget to practice the little courtesies. Politeness is to the finish of living as polish is to a fine piece of furniture. No matter how fine the wood, it does not make a fine piece of furniture in its unfinished state. In the same way, by failing to observe the common courtesies, we lose the polish which makes life smooth and pleasant. The words *please* and *thank you* cost us nothing and pay us much. Try to smile even when you are sad of heart; it will become a habit and will take you far by attracting the right vibration to you; it will change your whole outlook on life.

"Unto everyone that hath shall be given, and he shall have abundance; but from him that hath not shall be taken away even that which he hath." (Matthew 25:29) Don't take life too seriously. Remember we are here to learn a lesson, and we are not here for long. Live and let live. By being generous we receive the more. If you buy new clothing, give your old to those who need it. The old garments will be new to them and bring them joy. Clear out your closets and they will be filled. A closed hand cannot be filled.

Do not worry about tomorrow, for tomorrow, if it comes, will take care of itself. God has put plenty within reach of all who seek it in the right way. Those who wait for Him to toss it into their laps will have little, but those who cooperate with Him will be blessed abun-

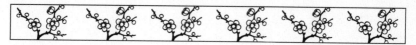

dantly. We are hear to learn, and the only way to learn is to work. So go out and gather in from near and far the bountiful supply that is yours to use.

> *Sweet sleep be with us, one and all!*
> *And if upon its stillness full*
> *The visions of a busy brain,*
> *We'll have our pleasure o'er again,*
> *To warm the heart, to charm the sight,*
> *Gay dreams to all! Good night, good night.*

T. B. Aldrich
Sleep

Dreams are the true interpreters of our inclinations, but art is required to sort and understand them.

William Shakespeare
The Merchant of Venice Act II

How I Met
My Chinese Teacher

Lee Ming

Many persons I meet want to know how I happened to take up the study of Chinese philosophy and the teaching of their religions. In the following I will endeavor to explain.

When I lived in China I was introduced, by an American friend, to a Chinese gentleman whose name was Kwan Tai Ching. Mr. Ching was wealthy, and like all wealthy Chinese men, owned a large estate about the size of one of our residential blocks. When I met Mr. Ching he invited me to his home to visit his family. I shall never forget the afternoon I went to his home for tea. After a short drive from my home, my chauffeur stopped at a large wall that had an opening just large enough for my car to pass through. The wall was all of two-and-a-half feet thick and twelve feet high and on top, embedded in the cement, were large pieces of broken glass which projected above the wall. As I had learned not to ask question while traveling in foreign countries, I made no comment. When I found myself inside the high wall and the gates were securely fastened, there greeted me one of the most beautiful gardens I have ever seen. Smilingly I looked about and was helped out of the car by one of Mr. Ching's servants and escorted to the big house that stood majestically in the garden. The servant at the door very politely escorted me through a spacious hall into the large front or receiving room. In the hall a massive hand-carved stairway of teakwood led up to the top floor. As this was the first Chinese home I had ever been in, it

was with some difficulty that I concealed my amazement, but I continued to smile and to give the impression that I was happy and pleased to be there.

The chair offered to me was dainty as could be, upholstered in brocaded pink silk, and the framework was light and hand-carved. To be sure, it was not very comfortable; but it was, as were all the other matching dainty pieces of furniture in the room, a masterpiece of art. I had no more than been seated than the servant left the room very politely, and closed the hall door silently. From another door, Mr. Ching made his appearance dressed in a gorgeous silk gown and a Chinese afternoon coat. Following him, bowing and smiling, was one of his six wives, the one that could converse in English. He greeted me by bowing and clasping his hands together, and so did his beautiful, cultured wife—for the Chinese do not shake hands. They think our custom of shaking hands is an awkward and uncouth way of greeting a friend. I do, too, since living in China. A gracious bow is so much better, cleaner, and nicer.

After this call, his whole family looked upon me as a friend. I spent many happy days in this home, and there learned much about the Chinese way of living. Their innermost thoughts were passed on to me as if I were one of the family. One of the events that happened while I was there was the engagement of Mr. Ching's eldest son. In China, when an engagement is announced, it is customary for the engaged couple to exchange presents, so I went with the Ching family to Soo Chow, China, where this was to be done.

As the Chinese really know the art of living, they make quite a celebration when one of their children is going to be married. The engagement party lasted ten days. All of us were put up in the best hotel in Soo Chow and the friends of Mr. Ching's family lavished

big, luxurious dinners upon us in their honor, as well as sightseeing trips and all sorts of shows and entertainments.

Mr. Ching's six wives and I would go over to a big temple in Soo Chow every morning, to Chin Chin Joss, as they called it. This was a paying of their respects to their choice saint and God. As I knew these ladies quite well by now, I could ask them anything I liked without embarrassment to either them or myself.

The first morning I went with them, I was amazed to see the large Chinese figures in the temple. Mrs. Ching, who spoke English, told me all about each statue as we lighted punk sticks to ask the spirits' blessing. She told me that these statues were not idols, as so many foreigners think; that each one of these statues represented the spirit of a saint that once lived in China and was sent by God to help the Chinese people, and that they did not worship them as idols. She said these statues were here so we would never forget them and so that when we were in trouble or in need, we could come here and ask their help. She said the Catholic church has its statues and pictures of its saints and they are used for the same purpose—to help them concentrate in prayer. She told me that some of the statues were 5000 years old, and led me down long rows of bronze figures, telling me the history of each saint as we passed along and placed incense sticks before them. She would tell me stories about a few every day. Before we left the temple we would throw some coins in the big box that stood in front of the high altar. I think this system of collecting money for the church is so much nicer than ours because it does away with the embarrassment of having a collection basket put in front of you at church while the congregation nearest you watches to see how much you contribute.

At this joss house, or temple, I met a Chinese priest. His name was Low and he welcomed me the same as the Chinese

ladies. He had a small square board on which was a design composed of little squares. He closed his eyes in meditation. Then he wrote in Chinese characters on a small piece of paper and handed one to each of us in turn. Mrs. Ching interpreted what he had written for me. To my amazement, everything he predicted happened that day.

I became so interested in this priest's strange powers that I asked Mr. Kwan Tsi Ching about it. He went into great detail to explain that these temple priests were men who lived good lives and who had studied to commune with the spirits that had passed on. He also said he knew a priest in Shanghai where he lived, who advised him on every business transaction he made. If the priest said it would be prosperous, he would make the deal, but if the priest said it would fail, he would let it go by. He told me that by taking the priest's advice he had made millions of dollars, and in appreciation for that advice he supported a large orphanage, a church, and his immense household. He then went into great detail to tell me how much rice was cooked and consumed in his large community kitchen. I was astonished to find out how many relatives and friends he supported. He also told me that his religion meant "love thy neighbor." I told him that I would like to study under one of these temple priests and learn his secrets of prediction. Mr. Ching said if I was serious he would arrange it, but that there would be hard work and many trials if I was to learn their way of thought.

When the priest at Soo Chow heard I wanted to study his religion, he said he would send a brother priest to teach me. So one day soon afterward, my head servant came to me and announced the arrival of the priest. My servant looked at me very inquisitively and said in pidgin English, "This man said he sleep on floor in servants' quarters, have got bed." I asked "Have you no bed for him?"

The boy said, "He no want bed. He sleep on floor. All same very poor man." I did not question my head servant, for I knew in the course of study with the priest, I would find out why he wanted to sleep on the floor.

My study with the pleasing, refined old priest began. I never knew a man could be so close to God. I learned the art of concentration and learned not to think evil thoughts and all the other fine teachings that went with this religion. He taught me that one of the most beneficial things was not to hate anyone, for hate is a deadly poison.

In the course of my studies with the kindly old priest, Lee Ming, I learned many things that I shall never forget and also acquired a philosophy that money cannot buy. He would sit on my big porch in the warm summer evenings, sipping tea, and tell me of the things that were to happen in the next hundred years, warning me to look for this or that which was to happen. He remained at my home for three months. Upon leaving he would not accept a penny from me, so I insisted on making a donation to an orphanage with which he was closely connected; also to his temple. Later, during a trip to the United States, I bought some American dolls, dressed them myself, and sent them to him for the children in his orphanage. Afterward I went to the orphanage and saw the little Chinese children cherishing those same dolls. It would have made anyone's heart jump with joy to see the happiness a foreign doll could bring to one of those little children.

When I returned to America I never forgot Lee Ming's teachings, and now, in our troubled world, I will try to pass his teachings along.

The reason I was inspired to make the fortune-telling game, *Gong Hee Fot Choy*, was to give the American people a little of the fine philosophy of the ancient Chinese.

Lee Ming died in China in 1928, a very old man, and Mr. Kwan Tsi Ching died in 1932. The night Mr. Ching died, the vision came to me that he called me on the phone and told me of his coming death. A few weeks later a letter came from China telling me he had passed on. To me they are not dead—they are alive and they often visit me, and Lee Ming urges me to write his teachings so he can help my people.

Numerology

Many people asked me, when they learned I was preparing a dream book, whether the subjects appearing in their dreams couldn't also be interpreted numerologically. Indeed they can, and the number associated with each dream subject or symbol (or combination of subjects) can be taken as the dreamer's "lucky" number for the next day or two following the dream.

You will see that each dream subject in *The Meaning of Your Dreams* is followed by a number. To arrive at this number an alphabetical-numerical table, in which each letter of the alphabet is assigned a number from one to nine, is consulted:

A	B	C	D	E	F	G	H	I
J	K	L	M	N	O	P	Q	R
S	T	U	V	W	X	Y	Z	
1	**2**	**3**	**4**	**5**	**6**	**7**	**8**	**9**

Therefore, if you dream of a cat, you can turn to this table and translate the letters C-A-T into the numbers 3-1-2. These numbers added together equal 6. Thus 6 is the number to pay heed to in the next twenty-four to forty-eight hours following a dream in which a cat figures prominently. Should you dream of more than one

subject, as one most often does, you would determine the one-digit number for each subject in the way I have described; add those numbers together and then reduce them to a single-figure number. If you dream of a dog as well as a cat, you would add 4 and 6 and 7 to equal 17. Then you would add 1 and 7 to equal 8. Then you would add Dog's 8 and Cat's 6 to get 14. Finally, you would add 1 and 4 to get 5. Thus 5 would be your lucky number for the next two days, a number to look out for.

No matter how many dream objects occur in a single dream, you can always determine your single-figure lucky number in this manner. I have done the calculating for all the dream subjects included in this book, but no matter what you dream, you can use this table to determine a lucky number.

The Meaning
of Your Dream

▾ A ▾

Abacus (2—The union of family or friend)

To dream of an abacus indicates you have or will have a condition in your life soon that will puzzle you. To dream you can use an abacus or are learning to use one means you will overcome your future obstacles and profit by same.

Abalone (7—A lucky dream)

To dream you gather or see abalone indicates you will have many secrets. If you eat abalone someone will confide secrets to you.

Abandon (6—Some new door opens)

To dream someone leaves or abandons you indicates that you are worrying or will worry needlessly over the past. To dream that you abandon someone or something means the end of worry or some disagreeable condition in your life.

Abbey (8—Money given unexpectedly)

To dream of an abbey indicates that you are in need of concentration on all matters to direct your affairs wisely.

Abdicate (9—An old condition ends)

To dream that you have to leave or give up something indicates that you should not be weak in your waking hours. Insist upon your rights in your future dealings.

Abduct (6—Mixed emotions—relax)

To dream that someone abducts you indicates someone will try to force you into some position or proposition that you dislike. If you dream that you escape, you will handle the situation to your advantage. If you do not escape, it is a warning to be careful of your affairs. If you dream that you abduct someone, do not force a future issue, as it will not be best for you.

Abhor (8—Someone will ask you for a loan)

To dream that you abhor someone or something happens that is distasteful to you is an indication that you will meet with some condition of this kind which will be beyond your power to eliminate. If this dream involves someone you know, their thoughts are not always the best toward you.

Ability (6—A new position, promotion, or business)

To dream you have great ability indicates that you should put this into practice. Choose something you like and stick to it, and your future success will be assured. To dream you have no ability means that you are either doing too much daydreaming or are sending your thoughts in the wrong pursuit. Concentrate; be more definite in your decisions.

Abortion (4—Suspicious friends)

To dream you have an abortion indicates the loss of prestige and name. Be careful after such a dream.

Abscess (5—Choose food carefully)

To dream of an abscess on yourself or someone near you is an indication than an unpleasant condition or situation is ending. This symbol always indicates a better money condition in the near future.

Absent (6—Privacy will be conducive to you)

To dream that you absent yourself without telling others where you are going indicates that someone is trying to pry into your affairs. To dream of absent friends means that they will return soon or you will hear from them.

Abundance (2—Comfort coming to you)

To dream that there is an abundance of anything in your possession indicates that something you are doing will turn out better than you expected. To see an abundance of anything means a new undertaking coming to you soon.

Abuse (3—Some past happening in your life is disturbing you)

To dream that you are abused indicates that something will cause you to worry and you will be depressed and very blue.

Academy (7—A gift of new magazines or books)

To dream that you see or attend one indicates that you will learn something to your advantage very soon. Also indicates that you are in need of more knowledge to help you succeed in the future.

Accident (5—Be careful in the street)

To dream of an accident happening to you indicates that you will have an argument. If you witness an accident it means that you will hear someone else argue. Also this dream warns you to be careful so that you may avoid an accident.

Accommodate (3—Someone will want to borrow)

To dream that you have to accommodate people you dislike indicates that someone will try to impose upon you. To have others accommodate you means that someone will repay you. To travel and find your accommodations poor indicates that you will have difficulty in making your living. Good accommodations mean that your living will be rosy for some time to come.

Accomplish (9—Good luck in store for you)

To dream that you accomplish a difficult task indicates a reward in the future for work well done, and also honor will be bestowed upon you. If you dream that you cannot accomplish what you set out to do means obstacles, or a disagreeable condition will be overcome by sheer grit and perseverance. Don't give up if this condition exists at present.

Accordion (7—The end of restricted conditions)

To dream you hear or play this instrument indicates that you will have to work, play, and give much to gain happiness.

Account (5—You waste your time in some way)

To dream that you have an account at a store indicates you should be careful how you spend your money. To have to give an account of your time to someone else means annoyances and petty worries will assail you. To demand someone else to account to you for their time means that you are not spending your time in the most profitable way.

Accused (2—An untrue friend or relative)

To dream that someone accuses you of something you did not do indicates that someone you have trusted is untrue. For you to accuse someone indicates that you should be on your guard, as a dream like this indicates there is something that you should know concerning the party you accused or the one who accused you.

Acid (8—You will burn a hole in your coat)

To dream of acid indicates for you to beware of someone's sharp, cutting remarks; you will be hurt by their angry words.

Acquaintance (4—You will attend a party)

To dream you make the acquaintance of noted people means some very enjoyable situation is at hand. To dream that you dislike a new acquaintance means you should beware of someone you will or have just met.

Acquit (5—A court action, or you will sign a paper)

To dream you are acquitted indicates the end of a financial burden.

Acrobat (6—You will soon meet blowhard)

To dream of an acrobat indicates that you will overcome many obstacles in the near future and will profit by them. Beware of relatives or friends who applaud your success but who would never lend a helping hand, as these are indicated by this dream.

Acting (9—Popularity is awaiting you)

To dream you are acting in a play indicates you will be called upon to do something in the near future that pleases you; or you actually will be in the limelight in some way.

Activity (1—You should go in and win)

To dream you are very active is a good omen. To be around much activity means a brighter outlook in the future or in whatever you are doing.

Actor (3—A bright proposition will be offered like the pot of gold…but it will be brass)

To dream you are a famous actor indicates you have ambitions that only perseverance will enable you to realize. Also indicates you have great desires. To talk to or see a famous actor means you truly have met the spirit of this actor during your sleeping hours.

Actress (4—Beware of a new friend)

Read actor.

Adapt (6—A tedious task in store)

To dream you have to adapt yourself to others' ways indicates servitude is in store for some time to come. But if you dream you have to adapt to a new job or position, you can expect better times soon. To dream you have someone around you who adapts himself to your ways indicates that prosperity will come to you through the cooperation of others.

Addicted (5—Tasks in store that annoy you)

To dream you are addicted to a habit of some kind indicates worry or shows a weakness in your make-up that should be corrected. To dream someone else is addicted to a habit of some kind means you will be annoyed at the way someone acts.

Adieu (4—A new door opens)

To dream that you say good-bye to someone indicates you should be careful of an accident. Good-byes are not a very good omen.

Adjust (3—Gain through adjustment)

To dream you are sent to adjust a bill or you do adjust one indicates you will finish something you wanted done for a long time. An adjustment of any kind means a loss or gain according to the way you dream about it.

Administer (4—Plenty of work for you)

To dream you administer aid to someone hurt indicates you will be called upon to do a favor for someone. To have someone administer something to you indicates gain. To be an administrator of an estate means you will be called upon to do a thankless job by thankless people.

Admire (5—A desire fulfilled)

To admire someone or something in a dream indicates you are longing for something you want. If you dream someone admires you, be careful of flattery and deceit.

Admission (4—A theatre party)

To dream you gain admission to a place of amusement without paying indicates you will be invited to a place where you will enjoy yourself.

Admit (2—Worry over fancied troubles)

To dream that you admit something means to be careful of what you do, as you may be watched.

Adobe (9—A new home in the future)

To dream that you see an adobe house indicates that you will face the hard facts of life with faith and hope. Adobe mud means you will have a hard time financially, but in the end you will win.

Adopted (2—You are lonely)

To dream of adopting someone indicates coming financial burdens.

Adorn (7—A good shopping trip)

To dream you adorn yourself in a beautiful array indicates that a good time and happiness are in store for you. Also you will buy some new clothing.

Adultery (7—A short illness)

To dream you commit this act indicates you will be lied about. Also see that your actions are above question. To dream someone else commits adultery means you should not listen to all you hear.

Adversity (5—A new world opens for you)

To dream you meet with adversity indicates you are worrying. If this is the case and you dream about it, you should concentrate on things better. Know there is plenty here for you, and you must have your share.

Aerial (1—You should follow your hunches)

To dream of a large aerial indicates you should develop yourself to receive the thoughts of others.

Affiliate (6—A business proposition soon)

To dream you affiliate with someone means you will be mixed up in something you want to do—sort of undersided; or you are lacking in a decision of some kind. The need of concentration is indicated here.

Affinity (9—You will be called upon to make a vital decision)

To dream you have such a person indicates gossip. If you truly have an affinity, a dream of same is a forerunner of bad luck. To dream of an affinity of any kind is a bad sign.

Affliction (5—Worry over nothing)

To dream you are afflicted with some terrible disease or ailment and you really have none indicates you need to change your way of thinking. If you are really afflicted, think of health and you will get it.

Affray (3—Unpleasant callers)

To dream of an affray, if mixed in it or not, indicates enemies.

Afraid (3—Be brave in your waking hours)

To dream you are afraid indicates you are being warned that all is not well. To see others who are afraid means you will have courage when it is needed. Also you may be persecuted.

Afternoon (9—An unpleasant task finished)

To dream it is afternoon indicates something important is to happen. Something very important will happen soon in the afternoon.

Age (4—Prosperity with age)

To dream you do not show your age is a good dream. To dream you are old and wrinkled indicates worry and dissatisfaction in your work or in the place you live. To dream of old people indicates long life.

Aggravate (1—Be careful of a cut or burn)

To dream you are aggravated by someone's actions indicates the ones you dream about are not the friends they pretend to be. To dream you aggravate someone, you should curb your ways.

Aggressive (4—You will hurry to catch a car)

To dream you are aggressive or around someone who is indicates you will encounter some very common people who will try to use you for their gain. To dream you are aggressive indicates for you to slow down.

Agitate (9—Enemies, gossip)

To dream that you hear someone agitating a crowd of people to strike or speaking to a crowd of people on any agitating subject indicates something will annoy you until you lose heart in whatever you are doing. To dream you are agitating something indicates you had better have care in your waking hours.

Agriculture (9—A growing fortune)

To dream you are farming indicates you will be very happy and prosperous in the future. To dream of agriculture in any form is good.

Aid (5—You will help with entertainment)

To dream you aid someone indicates you will be blessed for a good deed you do. To have someone aid you means you might want if you do not handle your money wisely.

Aim (5—Go in and win)

To dream you have an aim in life is a very fine dream; cultivate one in your waking hours. To aim at something, to throw or shoot, means to be straight and forward in your dealings with others. It will reward you in the end. To see others aiming, especially at you, means someone will criticize you.

Air (1—You will hear good music soon)

To dream of good fresh air indicates success. To dream the air is foggy, dirty, etc. means bad days ahead of you.

Airplane (6—A hasty trip soon)

To dream of an airplane indicates you will receive hasty news or callers, or you will make a hasty trip. Something hasty will happen soon in your waking hours.

Aisle (1—You will be proud of some achievement soon)

To dream you are walking down the aisle of any theater or church indicates you will be in the company of someone you will be proud of.

Album (4—You are retarded by living in the past)

To dream you see or look through a picture album indicates you will recall the past with old friends. If it is an old-time album containing dead relatives' pictures, they are wanting you to remember them.

Alibi (6—You should try to work more)

To dream you give an alibi is an indication that you should take care in what you do in your waking hours. To hear others giving an alibi means to be careful of lies.

Alkali (1—You should be careful of medicine)

To dream the ground is covered with alkali warns you to be careful of your money, as you might come to want.

Allegiance (6—A good dream)

To dream you swear allegiance to the flag, you can look for honor to be bestowed upon you.

Alley (1—Care in buying land)

To dream you walk or drive through an alley indicates you should be careful to do everything on the square. To see others in an alley means you should be on your guard or you will be cheated.

Alligator (5—You will meet a swindler)

To dream you see an alligator indicates strength and health. If it chases you, read about the meaning of dreams in front of book.

Allusion (4—A misrepresentation, caution)

To dream you see a beautiful allusion indicates you should investigate thoroughly anything pertaining to business in your waking hours.

Almanac (9—Time limited on a business deal)

To dream you consult the almanac about days indicates that you should try to spend your time more profitably. It means also that you may be wasting your time.

Alphabet (2—You will do intricate work soon)

To dream of the alphabet indicates that you are in need of more knowledge.

Altar (See Church)

Amateur (7—Progressive work ahead)

To dream you are an amateur at any undertaking indicates a new adventure is coming your way. To listen to or see amateurs indicates you will have new views on life.

Amazon (7—Aggressiveness by another)

To dream you see a large woman indicates you should strive for larger accomplishments in business, work, or art. Expansion of some kind is needed by you.

Ambition (2—You will be enthused soon)

To dream you are full of ambition indicates future good health

Ambulance (9—Help from unknown source)

To dream you see or ride in one indicates danger; be careful while on the street.

Amethyst (See Jewels)

Ammunition (3—You waste your energy)

To dream of ammunition in any form indicates loss.

Amputate (7—Severance of friendship)

To dream you see an amputation or hear of one, yours or someone else's, indicates danger, loss, or separation. On the whole this is an unpleasant dream.

Analyze (3—A new proposition offered)
To dream you or someone is analyzing anything indicates that strange facts will be revealed to you soon.

Ancestors (6—Spiritual help near)
To dream of your ancestors indicates they want you to remember them and to think of them often.

Anchor (3—Wasted time)
To dream of an anchor of a boat or that you anchor something indicates that you are not progressing fast enough.

Ancient (3—Lasting happiness)
To dream of an ancient place or thing indicates it will take time to accomplish whatever you are doing or going to do, but in the end it will be recognized.

Angel (3—A good dream)
To dream of an angel indicates that happiness comes through being kind to others.

Anger (9—Dissatisfaction)
To dream you are angry or see others angry indicates you will have something come up soon that really will make you angry. Guard against this if you can.

Animals (6—A good dream)
When God created life upon the earth, He created the animals for man. We know that whatever God created was good; therefore a dream about animals of any kind is a good dream. Many people think that a dream about an animal of which they are afraid, such as snakes, is a bad dream, but this is not true. If the animals in the dream, no matter what kind of animals, are in good condition, the dream is a good omen; if they are in poor condition, the dream is a warning and should be given special attention. Please read the story of Pharaoh's dream (Genesis 41: 18–21, 28–31). The seven fat cattle stood for seven good years, while the seven lean cattle warned of seven years of famine. To dream of being chased by an animal warns of a treacherous enemy.

To dream of any kind of domestic animal is a good dream. It indicates prosperity and an addition to what you own. Cows in a pasture indicate contentment; horses indicate good luck, prosperity; cats indicates enemies that pretend to be friends; dogs indicate love and loyalty; young puppies indicate many happy hours in store for you. Young animals indicate the new things that are coming. Old animals as a whole are good luck. Wild animals of any kind mean ungrasped opportunities. As a whole, animals indicate coming opportunities; grasp them.

Animals Used for Work (7—Help from others)

To dream of any animal which is used for work, such as the horse, donkey, elephant, or camel, indicates friendship.

Anniversary (2—You lament too much on the past)

To dream of an anniversary, yours or another's, indicates you are wasting time. After such a dream make a mental check of yourself; concentrate and see if you are doing all you can.

Annoyance (2—You take life too seriously)

To dream you are annoyed or you annoy someone else indicates this condition will arise. Be careful of your actions after such a dream. If you are annoyed at what you hear, you will truly hear something that will annoy you.

Anthem (7—Loyal friends)

To dream you sing or hear a country's anthem indicates that rumors of war are imminent.

Antidote (7—False friends)

To dream you administer an antidote or take one yourself indicates that someone will talk about you, and you will make them retract their lies.

Antiques (7—A legacy coming)

To dream of antiques indicates that a better living condition is coming into your life—better times from past endeavors.

Antiseptic (8—Retracted steps)

To dream you use same or apply it to someone else indicates you will be obliged to combat gossip.

Antlers (8—A trip to the country)
To dream of antlers of a wild animal indicates hard times and lost opportunities.

Ants (9—Small bills to pay)
To dream of ants indicates petty gossip, trouble, worry, and small annoyances.

Anvil (4—Good achievement near)
To dream of a blacksmith's anvil indicates that through hard work you will achieve whatever you have set out to do. To see an anvil in use and sparks flying from same is the sign of a brighter future for you.

Anxiety (8—Relaxation is needed)
To dream you are very anxious indicates there is something coming soon that will make you so. This dream is a forerunner of anxiety of some kind.

Apartment (9—Suppressed desires)
To dreamy you occupy a nice apartment indicates contentment. To dream you are moving into a new apartment means you will have a mixed, unsettled mind for some time to come.

Ape (4—Mockery)
To dream of an ape indicates that you should not imitate others, but do things in your own individual way.

Apologize (7—Be brave)
To dream you apologize to someone indicates you will be imposed upon. To apologize shows a weakness in your waking hours; curb this.

Apostle (7—A blessing for you)
To dream of one of the Apostles of the Bible indicates you will receive a blessing from the Apostles if you will ask for it.

Apparel (6—Good luck soon)
To dream you are beautifully dressed indicates good luck, good times. To be dressed in white is one of the best dreams you can have—white is excellent; red means love; blue means contentment to come; yellow means good luck in the future; brown means good work or position; black means sadness. The better you are dressed, the better the prosperity.

Appendix (8—You complain too much)

To dream of your appendix or someone else's indicates your thoughts need changing; think always of good health.

Applaud (8—Something new for you)

To dream you applaud or someone applauds you indicates you will be chosen to do something that brings you before the public; or you get a better position—a better condition is indicated here.

Apple (See Fruit)

Apprentice (8—You will do new work soon)

To dream you apprentice yourself to learn a trade indicates coming opportunities.

Apricot (See Fruit)

April (2—Buying or selling is good)

To dream it is April indicates coming opportunities through something pertaining to the earth, such as agriculture, mining, oil, or land investments.

Apron (1—You should be neat; it pays)

To dream of an apron indicates someone will try to cover up or hide something from you that you should really know. Be alert and find out something to your benefit.

Aqueduct (2—Money laid away for the future)

To dream of a water supply indicates play is in store for you in the future. Good luck will flow into your lap.

Arch (3—You will visit a place of grandeur)

To dream of a large archway indicates you will soon be inspired by a happening to do better work and greater things.

Archer (8—Aim high, you will succeed)

To dream you take up this art or see someone who is an archer indicates you should try to improve your methods of doing work. A lack of efficiency is indicated.

Architecture (5—Big plans for the future)

To dream you are an architect indicates that your plans for the future are well founded. If you talk to one, it means you will plan with others to go on a pleasure trip. Beautiful buildings mean a better future.

Argue (7—A dissatisfaction)

To dream you argue with someone indicates you will have an argument. To hear others argue means you will hear something you will disregard.

Arithmetic (7—A legal paper signed by you)

To dream of figures indicates time. You should always try to remember the numbers you dream about, as they represent the number of days when an important event will take place in your life. If you try to figure up a column of numbers and can't, it indicates much uncertainty around you.

Arm (5—Loving help)

To dream of arms, yours or someone else's, indicates the support of loyal friends. To lose an arm means you will lose a friend. A sore arm means you will hear of a sick friend.

Armor (2—Someone will scare you)

To dream of old-fashioned armor indicates time ill spent.

Army (3—You will be in a large crowd)

To dream of an army indicates confusion. To dream you are in the army means there will be no change in your future welfare for some time. For a woman to dream of a marching army indicates power over people, especially men. An army to business men indicates a smooth-running organization.

Aroma (3—A good time in store)

To dream of pleasant odors or perfume is a very happy omen.

Arrest (7—A past event annoys you)

To dream you are arrested is a warning that you should be careful and avoid being arrested, or something very annoying will happen.

Art, Artist (3—Hidden talent)

To dream you are an artist or are interested in art indicates you should develop your talents. They will finally make money for you if you desire. Sometimes a dead artist will contact a person during sleep, and he will help you. After such a dream, cultivate any talent you have.

Art Gallery (3—Refined friends)

To dream you visit an art gallery indicates you will form companionships with refined people. The higher the art, the more pleasing will be the companionship. To buy or sell art indicates you should be careful of future investments. To dream of painting a picture indicates hard work ahead. Beautiful vases, lamps, or sculptured art indicate a better home.

Ash (1—A new future for you)

To dream of ashes indicates you should forget the past and start with new ideas, friends, etc. Ashes mean the finish of something in your life.

Asphalt (5—A sound prosperity)

To dream of asphalt or streets of same indicates much hard work is in store for you and much progress is evident. Your views will broaden as you go along. A favorable dream.

Assassinate (1—Scandalous news)

To dream of an assassination indicates a disaster near you or a great scandal you will read about.

Assault (3—An argument over a purchase)

To dream someone assaults you indicates you should be careful of an accident. To dream you hurt someone means you should control your temper.

Assembly (6—You should be calm)

To dream you attend a large assembly indicates confusion.

Astrology (6—New study for you)

To dream of reading your horoscope or that you are interested in astrology indicates that you should lay your plans now for the future, and there is quite a distance for you to go before you reach the success you are after. Also you will find your life and work interesting.

Asylum (1—You will be called upon for advice)

To dream of an insane asylum indicates there are some people around you whom you think should be in one. Also some ideas you have are of no value. Be sure you are following work you like best after this dream.

Athletic (6—You will garden if you have one)

To dream you like athletic activities indicates good health, prosperity. This is a good dream.

Atmosphere (3—You are dissatisfied)

To dream of a clean atmosphere indicates good times ahead. Foggy or murky weather means your affairs will be very uncertain. If you dream the atmosphere cleans up, good times will come after trouble.

Attic (1—Give and you shall receive)

To dream of an old attic indicates you should not neglect your affairs. This dream indicates neglect of some kind.

Attorney (1—You will sign legal papers)

To dream you employ an attorney, or that you are studying law or are an attorney, indicates a coming law suit.

Auction (2—You need to purchase something)

To dream you attend an auction indicates you will get a bargain in something you buy. If you are holding the auction, you can look for some loss, worry, or a broken home. This indicates scattered forces.

Audience (8—To professional people a new contract)

To dream you attend a show and there is a large audience indicates, if in business, good business. To a professional person, a large audience means wealth and popularity. A good dream. To other people it means pleasure to come.

August (9-An outing in the country)

To dream of the month of August indicates warm friendships and many good times in store.

Aunt (2—Money received unexpectedly)

To dream of an aunt indicates an inheritance.

Aurora (2—You should plan your own future)

To see an aurora indicates you should not be discouraged by false promises. Be careful what you hear, see, or do after this dream.

Author (2—You should make future plans)

To dream you are one or talk with an author is a good sign. It means there is something you will do in the future that you will accomplish through the reading of books. It indicates you require study.

Autograph (8—Visitors soon)

To dream someone wants your autograph indicates that you should be careful of any papers you sign in the near future. To look through an autograph album means fond memories.

Automat (1—Food for thought soon)

To dream you eat there indicates you may make a wrong move and lower your living standards. Be careful after this dream; it is not favorable.

Automobile (5—Take things slowly)

To dream you own one indicates coming success. To ride in one means hard work and few pleasures ahead. To wreck one means you should be careful of your affairs. There is a warning here for you; it also means don't try to slide over your work or affairs; if you do you will lose out in the end.

Autopsy (9—You are discontented)

To dream you are present at an autopsy indicates you are either following the wrong pursuit or are disgusted with everything in general. An upset mental or physical condition exists—discontent.

Autumn (6—New furniture or clothes)

To dream of a beautiful autumn indicates the coming of prosperity and that disagreeable things have passed.

Avenge (9—You need relaxation)

To dream you avenge some wrong indicates someone is an enemy to you.

Aviator (5—You will reach a high goal)

To dream you are an aviator indicates you should be careful if you have dangerous work. This is a warning of danger to you. To dream of a famous aviator on a long, dangerous journey means you will escape a terrible accident.

Awaken (1—A bright idea comes to you)

To dream you are awakened out of a sleep when you really are not is a warning to attend to something in your waking hours, or of danger of some kind. Be careful.

Ax (7—Sharp trading or bargains)

To dream of an ax indicates sharp bargains will bring you success. To be cut with an ax means be careful what you say about others. An ax is not a favorable dream.

Axle (6—A good dream)

To dream of an axle of any kind means support from others.

> *Oh! the perjury of men! I find that dreams do not always go by contraries.*
>
> Henry Fielding

▾ B ▾

Baby (3—An upsetting condition)

To dream of a baby indicates financial worries and trouble and sadness. I hate to tell you this about a nice, sweet baby, but when I have something of great importance to decide and I am bothered about a decision, a baby is ever present with me while I sleep.

Bachelor (2—Selfishness near you)

To dream you are a bachelor means you should beware of becoming selfish. Also indicates loneliness.

Back (8—A friend will return)

To dream of your back indicates you should watch those about you. You will gain valuable information.

Badger (1—A new purse or briefcase)

To dream you see a badger indicates loneliness.

Bag (1—You should save for the future)

To dream you have a bag full of something indicates plenty in the future for you. If it is empty, there is a loss.

Bagpipe (2—A theatre party)

To dream you hear or play a bagpipe indicates you are wasting time, or someone will talk so much to you that you will become tired—a blowhard.

Bail (6—Someone will ask you for a loan)

To dream of furnishing bail, or of securing bail for yourself, indicates you should use caution, as there is someone who wishes to use you for his own ends in a way which would be costly to you. This is not a good dream.

Bait (5—Money, but handle wisely)

To dream of bait for fish of any kind indicates trickery. Beware of something being falsely represented after such a dream.

Bake, Bakery (1—Pride in accomplishment)

To dream you are baking indicates you will achieve something soon that you will be proud of. If your baking turns out badly, don't be disheartened in your waking hours; things will be in your favor in the end. To dream of a large bakery indicates changes and prosperity.

Ball (9—A trip soon)

To dream you attend a ball indicates an invitation is coming your way. To dance with a nice partner while there means a sea voyage—pleasure mixed with sadness.

Ballgame (8—Retarded ambition)

To dream you play ball or attend a ballgame indicates life and energy. You are wishing or you are seeking too much pleasure.

Balloon (2—A misrepresentation)

To dream of a balloon indicates honor bestowed upon you. A surprise for you.

Bamboo (3—This is a good dream)

To dream of bamboo is an indication of long life.

Banana (6—A dinner party)

To dream of a banana or banana plant indicates money coming to you.

Band (3—You will attend a theatre)

To dream of a band indicates happiness. To dream you play in a band indicates many opportunities will come to you. This is a good dream.

Bandage (9—You see freedom from boredom)

To dream of a bandage indicates that you will be suppressed in what you want to do. This is not a very good dream.

Bandit (5—Caution should be used)

To dream of a bandit indicates that you should beware of thieves

Bank (1—Security in old age)

To dream of a bank, or anything or person pertaining to a bank, indicates future prosperity.

Bankrupt (4—You need new lines, if in business)

To dream you go into bankruptcy, or your business is failing, if this should be a true condition, indicates you should not act impulsively in disposing of your business, as time will take care of the situation. To dream of bankruptcy when your business is in good condition indicates that some people bear watching.

Banquet (8—Business deal at mealtime)

To dream of a banquet indicates that if the food is good and you enjoy yourself, you will have prosperity for some time to come. If you are disappointed in the banquet, what you have planned will not materialize up to your expectations.

Baptize (7—A blessing from heaven)

To dream that you are baptized or you witness a baptism indicates that you will tell someone you are going to wash your hands of some business deal. The turning of a new leaf in your life is indicated.

Barber (1—A new venture)

To dream you are a barber indicates that you will have to do some work or a favor for someone whom you dislike. To dream you are being barbered for a special occasion indicates that, if single, you will be married; if married, you will attend a wedding.

Barn (8—Plenty of work in store)

A barn full of hay indicates abundance.

Barrel (2—Fun and laughter)

To dream of a barrel, if full, indicates plenty in store for you. An empty barrel indicates you will have to hustle to make ends meet.

Basket (4—A friendly gathering)

To dream of a market basket indicates plenty through thrift. Fancy baskets, like a sewing basket, indicate pleasure and work combined.

Bat (5—A good dream)

To dream of a bat is good luck. To kill a bat in a dream is bad luck.

Bath (4—A good dream)
To dream of bathing in the bathtub indicates the closing of old undertakings and the beginnings of new ones. To bathe in a beautiful, clear river or large body of water of any kind indicates new opportunities, new prosperities. This is a very good dream.

Battle (6—This is not a good dream)
To dream of seeing or participating in battle indicates rumors of war.

Bay (1—Change and a trip)
To dream of a beautiful bay indicates that prosperity is in store. With ships sailing on same means many trips and changes for you. If the waves are rough, many ups and downs are in store for you. A very full life is indicated on the whole. A good dream.

Beach (1—Summer pleasure)
To dream of a beautiful, clean beach indicates pleasure and prosperity. With the waves gently rolling in, new opportunities will come to you in abundance. If the waves and ocean are rough, some of the opportunities will be difficult to handle. If the beach is dirty, it means hard work and struggle before you finally reach success.

Beacon (4—A spiritual help)
To dream of a beacon that guides the ships or airplanes indicates that a ray of hope guides you.

Beads (4—Love and friends)
To dream of stringing beautifully colored beads indicates varied tedious and small tasks will confront you. To pray with the rosary beads means a blessing.

Beans (3—You should change your thoughts)
To dream of a bean field, or of gathering, cooking, or eating beans, indicates hard times for the dreamer.

Bear (8—A good dream)
A bear indicates a new friend to be made.

Beaver (8—A new coat for you)
Indicates the purchase or gift of a new fur piece.

Bed (2—A wedding or birth)
To dream of a beautifully made bed indicates harmony. Beautiful bed

covers indicate hope. A beautiful bedroom means a change for the better in the future. A beautiful bedset with spacious drawers in the dresser indicates plenty coming your way. A beautiful bedroom is a good dream. A dirty, poor bed indicates that your lot will be hard for some time. A poor bedroom means poor management.

Bedbug (5—A loan paid)

To dream there is a bedbug in your bed indicates that a change is needed badly in your life. To kill bedbugs means you will overcome obstacles and profit by same.

Bee (3—Money)

To dream of the busy little bee is an indication that you should apply yourself diligently. The more bees, the more prosperity is in store for you.

Beer (3—Not to plan more than you can do)

To dream of drinking beer indicates you should beware of reckless waste.

Beggar (8—Waste)

To dream of a beggar indicates loss. Be careful of your purse after this dream.

Bell (4—Prayer)

To dream you hear a bell indicates danger. Wedding bells mean happiness. Church bells indicate a blessing.

Berries (4—Work and money)

To dream of gathering berries indicates tedious work ahead. To eat berries indicates coming luxury.

Betray (8—A friendly enemy, jealousy)

To dream that someone betrays you or your confidence indicates this will take place. Beware if you know the party you dreamed about betrayed you.

Betting (5—Do not waste)

To dream of betting indicates that "willful waste makes woeful want."

Bible (3—You need spiritual help)

To dream of the Bible, especially if you read it, indicates a blessing bestowed upon you. A good dream.

Bicycle (5—Slowly but surely success)

To dream you are riding a bicycle indicates that health and plenty of hard work are in store for you.

Bill (8—Slowly but surely you will succeed)

To dream you owe a bill or you worry about a bill indicates you should concentrate and clear up the worried condition that surrounds you. To pay a bill indicates you will finish a hard task.

Billboard (3—A new popular friend)

To dream of a billboard or the advertising thereon indicates popularity coming your way. Be pleasant to everybody.

Billiards (5—Want through pleasure)

To dream of playing billiards is a warning not to waste your time.

Bin (7—Money through thrift)

To dream of a bin filled with whatever it is supposed to contain indicates an inheritance. If the bin is empty, you will be disappointed in the amount of an inheritance you receive.

Birds, Bird's Nest (6—Good luck and money)

To dream of a beautiful bird of any kind is a good news omen.

Birth (3—A new position)

To dream of a birth indicates new opportunities.

Birthday (6—Time well spent)

To dream it is your birthday indicates you will receive a gift. To dream of someone else's birthday indicates you will have a gift.

Bishop (7—Solace from friends)

To dream of a bishop indicates you will be called upon to give alms.

Blackboard (6—A spiritual message soon)

To dream you write, or see writing, on a blackboard indicates that something hidden will be made known to you.

Bladder (1—You will hear exaggerated opinions)

To dream of a bladder, yours or another's, indicates annoying, inflated ideas. Don't take stock in what you hear in the next week.

Blind (5—You will investigate a new deal)

To dream of window blinds indicates hidden secrets that you will find out. To dream of a blind person indicates you will be called upon for sympathy. To dream you are blind means you will be deceived in business or a love affair.

Blood (3—An injury; be careful)

To dream of blood indicates sickness. Be careful after this dream; watch your health.

Blush (8—If single, a new love affair)

To dream you see someone blush indicates purity of heart. If you blush, you will be esteemed by others.

Boast (3—Be careful in conversation)

To dream you hear someone boast or you are boasting yourself indicates false hopes.

Boat (2—Smooth sailing, with plenty to do)

To dream you own a boat or go boating indicates you will attend a picnic.

Body (1—Good health and happiness)

To dream you have a good, strong body indicates you will be blessed.

Boils (3—Select your food carefully)

This indicates money and sickness.

Bomb (5—Disturbing vibration around you; relax)

To dream of a bomb indicates war.

Book (7—Take up a new hobby; it will pay)

To dream you see many books or are reading books indicates you need knowledge in whatever you are going.

Boots (8—A trip will be offered)

Borrow (6—You will be delayed)

To dream you borrow money indicates a loss. For someone to borrow from you indicates the loss of a friend. To borrow at all is a poor sign.

Bottle (2—Good luck is in store from past efforts)

To dream of fancy bottles means happiness. Bottles full of perfume indicate luxury and prosperity. Ordinary or commercial bottles indicate that many services will be rendered to you.

Bouquet (2—Happy days ahead)

To dream you receive a bouquet of flowers, if single, means a proposal; if married, an invitation to the theatre.

Bowling (9—Hard work to achieve)

To dream you are bowling or in a bowling alley indicates a swift completion of what you are doing if all the pins fall down. If a few stand up, you will have just that many obstacles to overcome before you reach success.

Box (5—Abundant future)

To dream of receiving a box indicates coming presents. A beautiful box, new clothing.

Bracelet (See Jewels)

Bread (See Baking)

Breath (9—Do not let others dominate you)

To dream that it is difficult for you to get your breath indicates adversity.

Brewery (6—A good dream)

To dream of a brewery indicates money.

Bride (2—See wedding, a good omen)

To dream you are a bride indicates that much happiness is in store for you. To wear the dress of a bride means that good luck and social honor will be bestowed upon you. This is a good dream.

Bridge (9—Look forward, you will win)

To dream you cross a bridge, no matter if it is rickety, narrow, or long, and you reach the other side safely, indicates a complete change in your life and affairs. If the bridge breaks down or you turn back, it means trouble.

Bronze (8—You will buy a lasting object)

To dream of bronze, any object, indicates wealth coming your way.

Broom (9—Evil thoughts from others)

To dream that you sweep with a broom indicates worry and trouble and gossip, petty jealousies; but in the end, you will sweep them all up and get rid of them.

Brother (4—Friendly help from others)

To dream of your brother indicates support from your family.

Bucket (7—The fulfillment of a hope)

To dream of a bucket of clear water indicates health. A full bucket of anything else indicates gains.

Buddha (4—Spiritual help)

To dream of a Buddha indicates wealth, health, and happiness. To dream of a broken Buddha indicates a death of a close relative or someone you love dearly.

Buffalo (9—Someone will help you with a burden)

To dream of a buffalo indicates a loyal friend.

Buggy (8—A good dream)

To dream of an old-fashioned buggy indicates that prosperity will come slowly but surely.

Bugs (4—In an orchard, plentiful harvest)

To dream of bugs indicates petty annoyances.

Buildings (See Architecture)

Bunting (5—You will attend a picnic or celebration)

To dream of bunting indicates patriotism.

Buoy (9—Care in travel)

To dream of a buoy indicates you should take great care in your business dealings, your work, or in anything you do during the next week.

Burden (1—Check your attitude toward work)

To dream you are loaded down with a burden of some kind indicates overwork or sickness.

Burglar (See Thief)

Burr (5—A severed friendship for the best)

To dream you have a burr in your clothes, or thorns or stickers of any kind, indicates unpleasant visitors.

Business (9—Prosperity ahead)

To dream of business or that you are full of business indicates that if you hold the thought of business in your waking hours, good business or work will come your way.

Butcher (5—Tears will fall)

To dream of a butcher indicates sadness.

Butterfly (5—New gay clothing for you)

To dream of a beautiful butterfly indicates you will receive a beautiful gift.

Buzzard (8—The clearing up of a bad situation)

To dream of a buzzard indicates you will be forced to have dealings with a miserly, common person. This party will positively aggravate you.

> *A Friday night's dream on the Saturday told,*
> *Is sure to come true be it never so old.*

William Hone

▾ C ▾

Cabin (2—Be more aggressive and win)

To dream of a nice cabin in the mountains indicates promotion in your work or successful business. To dream that your home is an old run-down cabin is a warning for you to make more effort, so you can obtain the better things that are here for you.

Cable (5—Hard work and good health for you)

To dream of a strong cable supporting any large object indicates that you will have the support of loyal, staunch friends.

Cactus (4—Do not argue or fight)

To dream of a cactus indicates that you will have a strong enemy. This is not a good dream.

Cage (7—Unleash yourself and go forward)

To dream you are imprisoned in a cage indicates you are using limited thoughts. Birds imprisoned in a cage indicate delayed news. Wild animals in a cage represent ungrasped opportunities, and you are not acquiring the worldly possessions that are here for you.

Cake (See Bake)

Calendar (4—A good dream)

To dream of a calendar, with one month more prominent than the rest, indicates that something very fortunate will take place in that month. To dream that you consult a calendar and you remember the date indicated, something will take place on that date that is very important to you.

Calf (See Animals)

Call (1—Someone in the spirit world is helping you)

To dream you hear someone calling your name, if the party is dead that is calling you, indicates they want to commune with you and are trying to do so. To hear someone who is alive calling your name indicates hasty news. To have someone call on you indicates an invitation. For you to pay a call indicates you will have a party at your home and send out invitations.

Camel (See Animals)

Cameo (1—You will study ancient history)

To dream of a beautifully carved cameo or silhouette indicates a new admirer, if single; a lovely new friendship is indicated for married people.

Camera (5—Plan for the future)

To dream you own a camera indicates travel. Taking pictures indicates that the things you are doing at the present time will play an important part in building your future. To dream of taking pictures of landscapes indicates that at some time in your life you will own a farm. Taking pictures of your friends indicates they are thinking of you.

Camp (5—Rugged work is in store for you)

To dream you are camping indicates good health in the future.

Campus (1—Studio or a hobby soon)

To dream of a beautiful campus indicates that the knowledge you have gained in the past will be of great benefit to your future success.

Can (9—A dinner party postponed)

To dream of a can, like the can used for preserving foods, indicates a small gift is coming to you. The more cans, the better the gift will be.

Cancer (8—A gift of a twining plant)

To dream you or someone else is afflicted with cancer indicates there are damaging thoughts about you. Concentrate to clear this up.

Candle (3—Kind words will be spoken to you)

To dream of the soft light of a candle indicates future contentment and happiness.

Candy (2—A happy drive in the country)

To dream of candy indicates flattery. To lovers it means pleasant hours together.

Cane (5—Cooperate with others)

To dream you walk with a cane indicates you are depending too much on someone else. To dream you discard a cane means that a more independent and better future is in store for you.

Canopy (2—Pleasure and laughter)

To dream of a canopy indicates that happy days and much comfort are in store for you. To dream of a covered wagon means that hard times are ahead for you.

Canteen (7—The fulfillment of a hope)

To dream you use a canteen containing a good supply of water indicates future success. An empty canteen means many obstacles are ahead of you.

Captain (8—Not a good dream)

To dream of a captain on board ship indicates a coming sea voyage. To dream of a captain in the army indicates servitude and rumors of war.

Caravan (4—A slow move indicated)

To dream you are part of a caravan or see a caravan indicates that through striving for something new or trying to make a change you will meet with confusion. This is not a good dream unless it is an elegant, well-appointed, and well-directed outfit; then it means you will join with others in a large project, whereby you will meet with success and profit.

Cards (9—Relax and concentrate on what you want)

To dream you play cards indicates new opportunities will be presented to you. To tell your fortune by cards indicates there is something of importance you want to know and by right concentration you will find this out.

Carnival (8—A gift of a glass object)

To dream that you attend a carnival indicates that you will come before the public in the future in no uncertain way. This is a good dream.

Carpenter (3—You should buy a house or build one)

To dream of a carpenter indicates you will succeed in ridding your mind of petty worries.

Carpet (9—Comfort to come)

To dream of a luxurious carpet or rug indicates long life, comfort, and financial gains in the future. A ragged, dirty carpet is a warning that carelessness may cause a great disaster in your life, financially and otherwise.

Cartoon (5—Do not believe all you hear)

To dream you enjoy a cartoon in the newspaper indicates you should cultivate your sense of humor, and it will better your future success.

Cash (4—Investigate a new way to earn money)

To dream of cash, a cash box, or a cashier indicates coming danger. Be careful after such a dream.

Castle (6—A new home indicated)

To dream you see an old castle in the distance indicates you should not cultivate morbid desires. A beautiful new castle means that prosperity beyond your expectations is coming your way.

Cat (6—Be careful in handling a sharp object)

To dream of a cat or kitten indicates that someone you trust is not trustworthy, and this party will take advantage of you the first time an opportunity presents itself. This is not a good omen.

Catacomb (5—You will attend a funeral)

To dream that you visit the old catacombs in Europe indicates, if this dream is very vivid the next day, that you really visited this place in spirit. This has no definite significance, only the desire of your soul to want to see it.

Catalogue (4—A shopping trip soon)

To dream you look through a catalogue indicates that many opportunities are coming your way. If nothing attracts your interest while looking through it, you will blindly pass up these opportunities.

Cattle and Sheep (7—A good dream)

A dream about cattle or sheep is a good omen. A herd of good, fat cattle, sheep, or goats indicates money, entertainment, and travel. There is no better dream than a green field of fat cattle. But if the animals are poor and sick, look out for loss of fortune and sickness.

Cavalry (1—Horses are always good luck)

To dream of cavalry indicates that special protection surrounds you in time of need.

Cave (4—Protection in time of danger)

To dream of a cave indicates deceit. Something is being kept from you which you should know.

Cement (4—Plan a solid foundation for the future)

To dream of cement in any form indicates in the near future that you will meet with some hard, cold facts that will be difficult for you to decipher.

Cemetery (4—Follow your next hunch)

To dream you visit a cemetery indicates that someone who has passed on is trying to communicate with you. After this dream, relax upon retiring so this party may contact you.

Chain (8—Be more flexible in your opinion)

To dream of a chain of any kind indicates endless worries. The larger the chain, the greater the worry.

Chair (3—Comfort in old age)

To dream of a chair indicates financial, moral, or spiritual support in time of need. This is a good dream.

Chairman (4—Honor to close friends)

To dream you are made chairman of an organization, committee, or meeting indicates order, and also indicates that you should not waste your time.

Chalk (8—Forget the past; tomorrow is golden)

To dream you see or write with chalk indicates that great hopes you are holding will materialize into nothing.

Champion (7—Praise from loyal friends)

To dream of a champion or that you are a champion indicates that something you will do in the future will be more successful than you expected.

Chariot (2—You will meet a famous person)

To dream you see an old-fashioned chariot with beautiful horses indicates that you will profit by your old-fashioned ideas. This is a good dream.

Cheat (1—Be careful of a stranger—soon)

To dream you are cheated or are cheating someone indicates you are either careless or courting danger. A warning of care is indicated here.

Check (3—You will receive a loan)

To dream you receive a check indicates you should be careful of false promises.

Checkers (9—Money from many sources)

To dream you are playing checkers or see checkers indicates many new friends.

Cherries (4—A good dream)

To dream of picking or eating cherries indicates gain.

Chess (9—A card party invitation)

To dream of playing chess indicates you are wasting your time.

Chestnuts (3—A gift of fruit or candy)

To dream of chestnuts indicates some hard problems to be solved.

Chickens (See Fowl)

Children (1—You will hear of a birth)

To dream of children indicates worry.

Chimes (3—A blessing from Heaven)

To dream of hearing beautiful chimes indicates harmonious days ahead.

Chimney (2—A family gathering soon)

To dream of a high chimney indicates you will aspire to great things in this world. A chimney and fireplace in a home indicate domestic contentment in the future.

Chin (7—Do not be selfish)

To dream of a strong chin indicates strength of character and good health. To dream you are displeased with your chin means ill health.

Chocolate (1—If single, a new admirer)

To dream you eat or drink chocolate indicates flattery from the opposite sex.

Choir (8—You will attend a christening)

To dream of a choir, or of singing in a choir, indicates happy days and blessings ahead.

Choke (6—Do not listen to petty gossip)

To dream that you are choking or that you choke someone indicates you know secrets that someone is afraid you will reveal.

Christ (5—Divine love for you)

To dream of Christ or of His picture indicates that you are blessed. This is one of the best dreams that anyone could have, for your spirit to see or contact the Almighty Being. His spirit is seldom seen or contacted.

Christmas (9—A spiritual blessing)

To dream of Christmas indicates mixed joy and sadness. Also a family reunion.

Chrysanthemum (9—A good dream)

To dream of this flower indicates long life.

Church (7—A wonderful dream)

To dream of a church indicates that good luck and happiness are in the store for you. To dream you enter a church filled with grandeur means you will be inspired to greater achievements in life. To attend a church wedding indicates that you will be esteemed through your ways of administering justice to others. To attend a funeral at a church indicates the passing of worry and trouble and hardships. To dream of a church or anything pertaining to it is a good dream.

Cigar (See Tobacco)

Cistern (7—Look forward, not down)
To dream of a cistern indicates doubtful days ahead.

City (3—You will work with a large organization)
To dream you are in a large city means a confused state of mind. Also it indicates a change of some kind. Concentrate so that you will do the right thing at the right time.

Clairvoyant (5—You should listen to good advice)
To dream that you visit a clairvoyant indicates that there is actual contact with the clairvoyant while you slept and you should pay attention to the message received.

Clams (3—Be more generous with yourself)
To dream of a clam indicates that you should not be stingy or self-denying; there is plenty here for all of us.

Clay (5—You will buy or sell pottery or glass)
To dream of clay indicates the receipt of money.

Climbing (6—Do not listen to nagging people)
To dream of climbing a ladder indicates hard work in store. Climbing a hill and reaching the top indicates hard work with prosperity to follow. To dream of climbing but failing to reach the top indicates the frustration of your plans or that a retarding condition exists.

Clock (8—A big surprise for you)
To dream someone gives you a clock indicates a time will be set soon for some important event in your life; to a single person, a proposal. A clock also indicates slander.

Clothing (7—A door closes, another opens for you)
To buy a new dress, coat, or hat, or anything new in the line of clothing indicates happiness, prosperity, and honor. To dream of ragged clothes, or that you are ashamed of your clothes, indicates that you should guard against a slovenly attitude toward life in general.

Clouds (2—You will go to a funeral)
This dream indicates mourning.

Clover (See Hay)

Club (2—Much ado about nothing)

For a woman to dream she is very busy with club meetings indicates that her attention is needed in her home. For a man to dream of his club indicates loneliness. To form a club indicates you should keep your nose out of other people's business. To dream you attend club meetings indicates a dinner party.

Coach (3—A new business deal soon; change)

To dream you travel in a stage coach indicates retarded progress; in a beautiful railroad coach or bus, you are on the right road to prosperity.

Coal (4—Plenty indicated)

To dream you see coal indicates plenty in the future and many warm friends.

Coat (See Clothing)

Cobwebs (6—A young person, a new sweetheart)

To dream you see cobwebs is a warning to stay clear of the entanglements of others. Choose your company very carefully and the places you go.

Coconut (7—You will face hard facts gracefully)

To dream of coconuts indicates difficulties.

Coffee (4—Good health indicated)

To dream you are drinking coffee or see it or smell the aroma of coffee indicates disappointment and deceit from an unexpected source. This is not a good dream.

Coffin (8—A death in the neighborhood)

To dream that you select a coffin for someone you know indicates that this party may fill a coffin before long. Also to see a coffin indicates that there is an emptiness in your life.

Collapse (2—Look after your own business first)

To dream you see some object collapse indicates that you should attend to your own affairs and leave others alone.

College (5—Take up a hobby; it will pay)

To dream you are entering college indicates new investments, new enterprise, new opportunities are in store of you.

Comedy (See Theatre)

Comet (See Star)

Committee (2—Work and no gain, charity)

To dream of a committee or that you are placed on a committee indicates you will be called upon to give advice to others.

Communion (9—A blessing comes to you)

To dream you make your first communion indicates that great happiness is in store for you.

Company (6—You need a vacation)

To dream you have much company indicates popularity in the future. To dream that your company hinders or annoys you means you are blasé.

Compass (5—A goal will be reached by you)

To dream of a compass indicates that you are longing to make a trip. By the right concentration and planning you will accomplish your desires. This is a good dream.

Concert (5—You will go to a ball)

To dream you attend a concert or hear good music indicates an invitation to a very brilliant affair.

Confetti (2—If single, a proposal)

To dream of confetti indicates an invitation to an outdoor dance or a skating rink.

Conscience (9—The finish of an unpleasant task)

To dream that your conscience hurts you indicates, if you have done something that is not right in your waking hours, that you should not let the sun set until you have righted this wrong.

Contract (4—You will sign a legal paper)

To dream you contract to buy something or sign a contract indicates you should use great caution regarding any paper you may sign. This is a warning that care should be taken in this matter.

Convent (3—Study the Bible)

To dream of a convent indicates you will meet a refined, cultured person and will benefit by being in their company. To dream you enter a convent as a nun means you should be more religious or study spiritual subjects.

Convention (5—You will be in the limelight)

To dream of a convention indicates happiness, a meeting with an old friend, a family reunion, or that you will take part in something where there is a large gathering of people. To dream of attending a convention indicates good business, work, and honor in store for you, or the settlement of a perplexing problem.

Convict, Convicted (5—Ignore gossip you hear)

To dream you are a convict indicates that there is something in your past which worries your conscience. To dream you are freed indicates that you will be freed from this worry. To dream that you have been wrongfully convicted indicates that you are afraid of what people may say about you.

Cook (8—A good dream)

To dream you are cooking indicates your past endeavors will have something to do in forming your future. The more cooking and fussing you do indicates the more you will have to solder your past forces together to benefit your future.

Corn, Cornmeal (5—Rich living ahead)

To dream of corn or cornmeal indicates coming money.

Cornfield (5—Unexpected money)

To dream of a green corn field indicates that your endeavors will ripen into money.

Corns on Toes (3—You will buy new shoes)

To dream you have corns or calluses indicates retarded progress or that you will be taken advantage of by a friend or someone in your near family. This is not a good dream.

Corset (3—Change your style of dress)

To dream of a corset indicates you are surrounded by limited thoughts and suppressed in your desires. To dream you discard a corset means you will overcome such a condition.

Cosmetic (6—You will meet a dainty person)

To dream of cosmetics indicates that you should try to express beauty in everything you do. This will be to your advantage.

Cotton (6—Future stability)

To dream of fields of cotton indicates plenty. Cotton clothing indicates comfort and stability.

Country (8—Expansion in affairs needed)

To dream you are in the country and enjoying yourself indicates a change in your affairs or a move.

Court (5—Be careful if you sign a paper)

To dream you are in a court of law indicates that trials and tribulations are before you. Be careful of everything you do after such a dream, as you truly may end up in a real court. This is not a good dream.

Cousin (9—You will give a present)

To dream of your cousin indicates financial burdens.

Cow (See Cattle)

Coward (1—Deceit is evident)

To dream that you encounter a coward indicates you should have strength in your waking hours, as someone may harm you without your knowledge.

Crack (9—A break in life for the better)

To dream of a large crack in the wall, the ground, or a dish indicates a separation and a break coming in your life. If you mend a broken dish, you will take up an old issue where you left off or recover something that is rightfully yours.

Cradle (7—If a housewife, house cleaning)

To dream of a cradle indicates many cares in the future.

Credit (5—A good dream)

To dream you ask for credit and it is refused indicates you will be snubbed by someone you meet in the near future. To dream you have credit, or credit is offered you, indicates you are laying a substantial foundation for the future.

Cremate (2—A debt paid)

To dream of a cremation foretells the termination of something that has been worrying you.

Crepe (2—Need of a gayer dress)

To see crepe hanging on a door indicates a death in the immediate neighborhood. To wear crepe indicates you will shed tears.

Cricket (6—You will hear the sound of money)

To hear a cricket in a dream is a forerunner of good luck.

Criminal (7—Do not lament over the past)

To dream you are a criminal is a warning against an accident. To associate with criminals indicates you should choose your friends wisely.

Cripple (7—Change your outlook on life)

To dream of a deformed or crippled person or to dream that you are crippled indicates that something or someone is trying to retard your progress. After this dream be on the alert for any unexpected condition that may arise. This dream is always a warning that something is not right.

Crochet (See also Sewing)

To dream you crochet or see someone else crochet indicates that you should be careful that you do not become entangled in petty gossip and neighborhood scandals.

Croquet (8—If single and young, don't be too retiring)

For a young girl to dream she plays croquet indicates she might become an old maid. To dream of playing croquet indicates you should use more up-to-date methods in your business.

Cross (2—A blessing is coming)

To dream of a cross of any kind indicates faith. Also means victory over your trials and tribulations in this life.

Crossroads (5—You will make a wise decision)

To dream of crossroads indicates you will be undecided in a matter in the near future where two propositions will be offered at once. This is a good dream.

Crow (See Bird)

Crowd (9—If in business, great demands on you)

To dream of being in a crowd where there is pushing and shoving indicates hard work in the future, or a struggle to accomplish something that is important to you.

Crown (1—This is a good dream)

To dream that you admire a beautiful crown indicates coming power over others. To wear a beautiful crown means great happiness in store for you.

Crutches (7—Expand your views on life)

To dream of using crutches indicates that you are the kind of person who depends on others to do for you what you should do for yourself. If you are ill and dream of using crutches, the dream indicates that you will have a speedy recovery.

Cry (1—Your pent-up emotions need releasing; laugh)

To dream that you cry or see others crying indicates that you will feel badly or cry about something.

Crystal (8—A good dream)

To dream you look at crystal dishes, a crystal ball, or anything that is beautifully transparent indicates that you will make very fortunate decisions on any business proposition that is presented soon; or you will be very capable in the tasks set before you. You should hold a clear, direct thought on what you want after this dream.

Cupboard (8—A kitchen shopping trip)

To dream your cupboard is clean and well stocked indicates you will be well taken care of in your old age. To dream of a cupboard filled with beautiful dishes indicates that you will do much entertaining in the near future.

Cupid (8—If single, a proposal)

To dream of cupid indicates that someone will bestow much love on you.

Curse (3—You will meet a disquieting person)

To dream you hear someone curse or place a curse on someone indicates you will meet or contact something very distasteful soon.

Curtain (5—A change needed)

To dream of curtains indicates that you should not be too hospitable. Ragged curtains indicate slander.

Custom House (1—An unjust bill will be presented)

To dream you have your luggage passed through customs without trouble indicates a long trip by water for you. To dream you have trouble with customs indicates difficulty on a trip or in shipping merchandise. Be careful about shipping after such a dream.

Cut (8—Plan well ahead and go ahead)

To dream you cut your hand or person indicates someone will expose a secret you have. To cut out a dress or a pattern indicates that through planning you will make your future a success.

> *"And the Angel of God spoke unto me in a dream, saying 'Jacob': And I said 'Here I am.'"*
>
> Gen. xxxi, ii.

▾ D ▾

Dairy (See Milk)

Damage (4—Avoid an accident, be careful)

To dream that you see or damage something yourself is a warning that something around you is not right. Use care after such a dream.

Dance (9—If single, a trip with a new admirer)

To dream you dance indicates you will handle coming cares lightly. To dance with beautiful new shoes indicates a sea voyage. Dancing is a very good dream.

Dandelion (See Flowers)

Danger (4—Avoid hostile people)

To dream of danger warns you to be careful in your waking hours.

Darkness (1—Plan your affairs better)

To dream of darkness indicates that you should guard against doing things blindly without due consideration. Also you should look out for slander. There is something hidden from you you should know. Stop, look, and listen!

Daughter, Daughter-in-Law (3—A good dream)

To dream of a beautiful day indicates happiness; a rainy day, sadness.

Death (See also Funeral)

To dream of a death in your immediate family indicates unnecessary worry on your part. To dream you see someone else indicates that you really have.

Debt (4—Security established, honor)
To dream of bills you owe indicates they will be paid. To dream you are in debt when you are not indicates you should not worry, but should have confidence and the future will be well taken care of.

Deceive (7—Be careful of new acquaintance)
To dream you are deceived indicates you should be on your guard to prevent this.

December (1—A big change)
To dream of the month of December indicates a happy change coming into your life by the next December.

Decorating (4—A better condition ahead)
To dream you are decorating, remodeling, or reclaiming anything is a wonderful dream. It indicates prosperity, money, and that you will enjoy the better things of life.

Deed (9—You will buy or sell something)
To dream you do a good deed indicates you will have a good deed done unto you without your knowledge. A deed to property indicates prosperity and a fulfillment of a wish, worldly gains.

Deer (5—Love, if single)
To dream of this graceful, beautiful little animal indicates someone will bestow great love upon you.

Defend (2—You will give to charity)
To dream you defend yourself or someone else indicates a favor returned when you need it the most. To defend another means you will have to do a favor.

Delay (2—You will have a disappointment)
To dream of missing a train, boat, bus, or plane, or that you are having great difficulty packing, dressing, or preparing for a trip, or are frustrated in any way, indicates that you will be providentially prevented from doing something that would bring you harm.

Derrick (5—You will buy stock)
To dream of a derrick indicates that you will build great hopes for some undertaking or project.

Desert (8—You need more sunshine)

To dream of being in a dry, burning desert indicates that it will be a long time before you will make any money. To dream of vegetation flourishing in the desert indicates that you will start with little and make much.

Desk (3—Answer letter, someone awaits news)

To dream you have a desk loaded with papers indicates scattered energy in the wrong direction. To dream you have a clear desk means you will finish a task you set out to do, and you will benefit much by the same.

Devil (7—You will meet a devilish old person)

To dream of the devil, which we all know is a myth, indicates a warning that you should choose your company wisely. This is not a good dream.

Dial (8—Go in and win, try)

To dream of a sundial or the dial on the face of a clock indicates that it is trying to warn you that you are wasting valuable time.

Diamond (3—See Jewels)

Diary (3—Someone is watching you)

To dream of keeping a diary or reading a diary indicates that in the future someone or something will force you to give an account of your time.

Dice (3—Be careful)

To dream of throwing dice indicates many changes are in store for you. Good luck and bad luck mixed.

Dictaphone (5—Listen, make your own decision)

To dream of a dictaphone indicates you will find out someone's secrets, much to their dislike.

Dictionary (1—You will study a hobby)

To dream you consult a dictionary or see one indicates you should take stock of everything around you, as there is something you should know about.

Diet (2—Spend time outdoors, get sunshine)

To dream that you are on a diet indicates ill health.

Dirt (6—Clear your mind of old ideal)

To dream that things around you or something is dirty indicates that you will be very disgusted with something that happens after this dream. To dream you are cleaning a dirty place indicates the fulfillment of some desire.

Difficult (See Delay)

Digging (See Shovel)

Disaster (5—Be careful if you drive)

To dream of some great disaster indicates that this is a forerunner of some disaster.

Disease (9—Unwarranted worry; stop this)

To dream that you have a disease indicates that you should take care of your health.

Disgrace (2—You will hear gossip)

To dream that you are disgraced or have disgrace of any kind indicates you should pick your company wisely, as this is not a good dream.

Dishes (See Cupboard)

Disrobe (9—New clothing or toilet articles)

To dream that you disrobe indicates that you will discover the real facts of something you want to know.

Dive (4—A new business venture)

To dream you dive or see diving indicates you will plunge blindly into business or investments. If you see the diver swimming after the dive, the investments will be successful.

Divorce (4—Do not worry; cheer up)

To dream of a divorce indicates that care should be taken to prevent a loss or a separation. This is not a good dream.

Dock (See Wharf)

Doctor (3—Solace from a professional person)

To dream of a doctor indicates you will receive assistance from a source you least expect in time of need.

Dog (8—A good dream)

To dream of a dog, inasmuch as this animal is the mostly highly developed spiritually, is a warning or prophecy of some kind. These animals indicate friends or foes. To dream a dog loves you indicates love from your family or friends. To dream they snarl at or bite you indicates they are trying to warn you of enemies or approaching danger. A sick dog means sickness to a friend or yourself. Try to place your interpretation regarding a dream of a dog, so that you can place yourself as being the recipient of a message. To dream of a dog indicates good.

Doll (7—A new ornament for you)

To dream of a beautifully dressed doll indicates happy days are ahead of you. A broken or dirty doll means the loss of something valuable.

Door (7—Look into a new proposition soon)

To dream of an open door indicates you will receive a welcome from someone you least expect. A closed door indicates you will be an unwelcome guest and you will find out many secrets to your advantage.

Dove (See Birds)

Dragon (5—If in theatrical world, fame)

To dream you see a large dragon or any prehistoric or mythical animal is an indication of good luck. It also implies that you should endeavor to write your name in the sands of time. This is an encouraging and good dream.

Dress (See Clothing)

Drill (1—Be true to yourself)

To dream you are drilling or watching a drill working indicates that you should use strength and skill in your waking moments to cope with the things and work you have to do. This dream indicates that you should show strength in all matters of life.

Drouth (5—Be careful of a burn)

To dream of a drouth indicates war, pestilence, and plagues.

Drowning (3—Watch your cigarettes)

To dream that you are drowning or that you see another drown is a warning that you should beware of fire.

Drugs (6—You will visit a sick person)
To dream of drugs, herbs, or anything used in making drugs indicates you will be called upon to nurse someone.

Drum (2—If you drive a car, watch traffic signals)
To dream of hearing a drum beat indicates that you should be careful to avoid accidents in traffic.

Drunk (5—You will attend a basket)
To dream of being drunk or of seeing another in that condition is a warning to you against intemperance in your emotions, as well as in eating or drinking.

Ducks (4—Money you did not work for)
To dream of ducks indicates an inheritance for you, but trouble in collecting it.

Dump (9—Waste)
To dream of a large dump with all sorts of tangled refuse is a warning to take very good care of your health and business.

Dunghill (6—Health, wealth, and happiness)
This dream means money.

Dust (1—Do not listen to flattery)
To dream the air is full of dust indicates angry words. Also someone will try to do you a wrong and cover it up with smooth talk. Be on your guard after this dream.

Dye (7—A new suit or dress purchased)
To dream of dyeing anything indicates a change with profit for you.

Dynamite (1—Not a good dream, waste)
To dream of dynamite indicates war.

> *Come to me my darling; I'm lonely without thee;*
> *Daytime and nighttime I'm dreaming about thee.*

Joseph Brenan

▼ E ▼

Eagle (See Birds)

Ear (6—Laughable gossip)

To dream of an ear indicates news.

Earth (7—A very good dream)

To dream of clean earth indicates new opportunities are coming. To dig in a garden means prosperity. To dig a hole in the earth indicates you will unexpectedly discover something has been hidden from you.

Earthquake (8—Be careful of loss)

To dream of an earthquake indicates loss of property.

Eat (8—This is a good dream)

To dream you are eating indicates the fulfillment of some desire you have. To eat with others means enjoyment. To serve others while they are eating indicates gain through hard work.

Eclipse (6—A proposal, if single)

To dream of an eclipse of the moon or the sun indicates a decided change is coming in your life.

Eggs (2—Money through investment)

To dream you find a nest of eggs indicates you will make a discovery that will benefit you. Broken eggs mean you will lose something. To dream of eggs in general is a good dream.

Electricity (3—Unlooked for help)

To dream of using electricity in any way indicates you will receive strong support from others. This is a good dream.

Elephant (9—Good luck ahead)

To dream of an elephant indicates health and long life.

Elevator (See Climbing)

Elope (8—If single, a proposal)

To dream of an elopement, yours or someone else's, indicates that you should not overlook your obligations and surmount any obstacle in front of you. Don't shirk your responsibilities.

Embrace (2—Love from those you embrace)

When you dream that you embrace a loved one, you actually do so in spirit.

Embroider (See Sewing)

Emerald (See Jewels)

Empire (3—A vision from the past)

To dream you see a mighty empire indicates that one time in your past history you were the head of an empire and your soul has gone to visit its old place of inhabitance.

Empty (7—Careful to whom you make a loan)

To dream that you think a vessel is full but it really is empty indicates that a disappointment is coming your way.

Enemy (8—Take heed)

To dream you have an enemy indicates you really have one. Whatever you dream about the enemy, you can look for this to materialize in your waking hours.

Engagement (1—Be constant; it pays)

To dream you have become engaged, if single, indicates you soon will. To have any type of engagement indicates that you should be very exacting in whatever you do in the future. To break an engagement means lost esteem.

Engine, Engineer (9—Change for the better)

To dream of an engine or an engineer indicates that you will take a trip.

Entertain (7—A wonderful trip in store)

To dream you entertain or are entertained indicates happiness is in store for you.

Envy (See Hate)

Ermine (See Fur)

Errand (6—A long-standing debt paid)

To dream you go on an errand for someone indicates you will be asked to do something within a week. For someone to do an errand for you indicates someone will be very grateful to you.

Escape (4—You will escape an injury)

To dream you escape from jail or from someone who is pursuing you indicates victory over enemies.

Estate (7—You will receive a legacy)

To dream you inherit an estate, or are handling an estate, indicates that a will will be made in your favor.

Europe (8—Friends at a distance want you to write)

To dream you are traveling abroad indicates your soul really does visit there while you sleep, especially if you recall plainly the buildings and places where you thought you visited when you were asleep.

Exchange (4—Two opportunities for you)

To dream you exchange something indicates you will have two opportunities presented to you and you have a hard time deciding between the two.

Execute (2—The ending of a disagreeable situation)

To dream that you witness or read of an execution indicates the passing of something disagreeable out of your life.

Exhibit (5—You will buy furniture)

To dream of a beautiful exhibition of pictures indicates coming prosperity. This also applies to statuary or anything in the line of art.

Exile (1—You will be lonesome)

To dream you are in exile indicates that you will visit a jail, hospital, or some large institution. To dream you are forsaken by your friends or loved ones indicates you will be reprimanded for something you do or say.

Explode (9—Not a good dream)

To dream of an explosion is an indication you will receive startling information or news. The louder the explosion, the more people will be involved. This also applies to ammunition or anything capable of making a loud noise. Also indicates shattered friendships.

Explore (5—Go in and win)

To dream that you explore or are great explorer indicates that you should expand in your activities. The need of expansion is indicated here.

Exterminate (8—Moody)

To dream that you exterminate bugs or any kind of pest indicates you will cast aside petty worries, and by doing so you will gain in the future, as these small insects indicate money.

Extravagance (4—Buy what you need)

To dream you are extravagant indicates there is plenty here for you, and you should use all efforts to get this. This is a good dream.

Eye (8—A shrewd deal)

To dream of your eyes or someone else's indicates new friends. If there is something wrong with the eyes, your friend will have many faults. If the eyes are beautiful, a beautiful friendship is indicated.

Eyeglasses (9—Follow your hunches)

To dream you wear eye glasses or are fitted for them indicates there will be a change of outlook on your life.

> *Dreams are the true interpreters of our inclinations,*
> *but art is required to sort and understand them.*
>
> Montaigne

▼ F ▼

Fabric (3—New clothing)

To dream of beautiful fabrics indicates you should choose wisely in your waking hours.

Face (6—Plan and face hard facts)

To dream of a beautiful face indicates you will have a lovely friendship with someone. An ugly face means someone will try to use you for his gain.

Factory (7—A very good dream)

To dream you are in a factory humming with activity indicates opportunities, a new venture, and busy days ahead for you.

Failure (9—Do not worry; relax and work)

To dream that you are a failure indicates you lack concentration. There is success and plenty here for everyone. This dream means you should strive harder to succeed.

Fainting (8—Do not be deceived)

To dream of fainting or of seeing another faint indicates you should be aware of false friends.

Fair (7—Beware of fair weather friends)

To dream of attending a fair or participating in one in any way indicates that you will expend much money and effort with no return.

Fairy (5—Heavenly plans work well)

To dream of a fairy means good luck.

Faker (5—Be careful when you shop)

To dream of a faker indicates that care should be taken to avoid meeting with one.

Falling (7—Some food you have eaten disagrees with you)

To dream of falling indicates sudden loss.

Fame (7—A very fine dream)

To dream you are famous is a very good dream. This can be realized if you will put much effort in what you are doing. To dream you are with famous people indicates popularity.

Family (9—A burden lessens)

To dream you have a large family or of your family indicates that your assistance or financial help is or will be needed by them.

Famine (3—Plan wisely)

To dream of a famine indicates your spiritual help will be needed by many.

Fan (3—Frivolous company)

To dream of a fan indicates disputes.

Farm (2—A good dream)

To dream you live on a large farm indicates coming comfort and security.

Fat (Plan your diet wisely)

To dream you are fat indicates coming riches.

Father, Father-in-Law (4—Do not let others boss you)

To dream of your father or father-in-law indicates prosperous days ahead, and also support from your immediate family.

Fatigue (6—Relax; it will help you)

To dream you are tired indicates you need a rest.

Feather (9—Money, plenty of money)

To dream of feathers indicates light, flowery talk; foolishness.

February (6—You will buy new clothes)

To dream of the month of February indicates a change in your wardrobe.

Feces (2—Be careful in the street)

To dream you step in such indicates you will be called upon and forced to deal with repulsive, ignorant, common people.

Feet (8—Do not mix in others' troubles)

To dream that you have beautiful feet indicates that you will follow the right path to success. To have sore, crippled feet means that you will have many hardships and obstacles to overcome.

Fence (6—You seek privacy)

To dream of a high fence indicates you surround yourself with barriers of thought that keep you from succeeding as you should. To dream you are trying to climb a fence indicates better conditions in the future.

Fern (See Flowers)

Fever (2—Family troubles)

To dream you have fever indicates you will have an argument.

Field (9—Prosperity and money)

To dream of beautiful green fields of corn, wheat, hay, or any sort of vegetable or fruit indicates that plenty is in store for you. Dried, barren fields means you are lacking in concentration. Never hold a thought of poverty in your waking hours.

Fight (5—Sidestep a quarrel)

To dream of a fight indicates you should be careful in your waking hours.

Film (4—A beautiful new home)

To dream of a film indicates that what you are doing at present seems very blank now, but it will develop into something very beautiful.

Filter (7—Shun questionable people)

To dream of a filter indicates you must strive to separate the good from the bad. By so doing, prosperity is in store for you. This applies to friends as well as any endeavor you have.

Find (6—A gift for you)

To dream that you find something indicates a gift or a new discovery of some kind. To return to its rightful owner what you find indicates success through honesty.

Fine (7—Use care in your dealings)

To dream you pay a fine in court indicates care should be taken so that you do not lose a valuable. There is sort of a hidden loss indicated here.

Finger, Fingernails (5—You should take music lessons)

Beautiful fingers or fingernails indicate achievement.

Fire (2—Hold your temper)

To dream of fire in any capacity indicates the loss of prestige and reputation through the fiery words from an enemy's tongue. The greater the conflagration, the more loss you will have through the enemy's slander. Fire is not a good dream.

Fish (6—A good dream)

To dream of fish in any capacity indicates sharp bargains and money coming your way. Shellfish indicate secrets and profits. Scaly fish indicate money and good times. Fish, as a whole, indicate plenty.

Fishing (9—A good dream)

To dream you are fishing indicates that you should stick to one thing and not change from one thing to another. To catch little fish means success; big fish indicate big success. Not to catch any fish indicates you will be disappointed in money matters. To eat fish means knowledge is gained.

Flag (8—You will enjoy a great display)

To dream of a flag indicates that you will feel very patriotic. This is a good dream.

Fleet (3—A very good dream)

To dream of a large fleet indicates spiritual protection from your enemies.

Flood (7—Be careful of moths)

To dream of a flood indicates coming famine.

Flowers (8—A good dream)

To dream of beautiful flowers indicates romance. If single it indicates a wedding. Flowers indicate the addition of new relatives in the family. To dream of flowers on the whole is a beautiful dream for the future. This includes any kind of a plant, shrub, or blooming flower. They all represent new, beautiful things that are coming into your life.

Fly, Flypaper, Flytrap (7—Do not chase the butterfly)

This dream indicates that you will conquer your enemies and succeed.

Flying (See Aviator)

Flying (1—A trip by plane)

To dream of flying indicates that you should aim for the higher, more spiritual things in life. Through this a great change will come into your affairs.

Food (4—You will be invited to dinner)

To dream of well-cooked food indicates the arrival of unexpected guests. To cook and bake and prepare food indicate happiness and prosperity. Food, on the whole, is a very good dream.

Forest (2—A good dream)

To dream of a forest indicates great wealth. To dream of being lost in a forest is a warning that you should be careful not to waste this inheritance. If the trees are dead, or if a fire has swept the forest, this indicates loss of an inheritance or a dissipated fortune.

Fort, Fortress (5—Not a good dream)

To dream of a fort or fortress indicates war.

Fortune-teller (9—Spiritual help needed)

To dream of a gypsy fortune-teller indicates that you will be given bad advice. To dream of visiting a spiritualist medium indicates the need of advice.

Fountain (1—Beautiful days ahead)

To dream of a beautiful fountain with cool water flowing out of it indicates happiness and contentment of mind.

Fowl (2—Plan well; you will succeed)

To dream of chickens indicates a smooth-running home. Fowl of any kind is a very good dream. To kill chickens indicates worries. To cook and eat chicken mean desires will be fulfilled.

Fox (You will buy a new hat, if a male)

To dream of shooting a fox indicates that you will buy a new fur piece. To see a wild fox indicates you should beware of a cunning person.

Freckles (7—Scattered fortunes)

To dream of freckles on your face or someone else's indicates that the lot of the freckled person will be feast or famine.

Friend (2—A party and plenty of gossip)

To dream of a friend in need indicates you will be called upon to help a friend. To dream of friends in general is a very good sign.

Frog (1—If young, obey your elders)

To dream of a frog or toad indicates you should not disregard discipline from someone, as this is meant for your own good.

Frost (See Snow)

Fruit (2—A good dream)

To dream of any kind of fruit indicates health, wealth, and happiness in the future.

Funeral (5—There is a new position for you)

To dream of a funeral or anything pertaining to the dead indicates a great change is coming into your life. If you happen to weep at a funeral, it means you will be greatly disturbed over this change, but it will be the best for you in the end. To dream a friend of yours dies indicates someone you know will pass on.

Furniture (6—Lasting contentment)

To dream of beautiful modern furniture indicates good luck. To dream that your furniture is old and out-of-date indicates that because of a lax condition on your part, you are not getting the most out of life. Furniture is a good dream.

Furs and Fur-bearing Animals (1—Money)

To dream of fur-bearing animals indicates good fortune in store for you. If the animals are in good coat and the fur in good condition, you may expect good business and prosperity. To dream of killing these animals also indicates good times to come. To buy or wear beautiful furs in a dream indicates coming honors. To dream of beautiful furs indicates plenty.

We that are twain by day, at night are one.
A dream can bring me to your arms once more.

Lizette Woodburn Reese

▾ G ▾

Gamble (4—A new job for you)
To dream you are gambling indicates that you should not waste your time on games of chance. To dream you win means good luck is coming your way.

Garden (4—A good dream)
To dream you walk or work in a beautiful garden means contentment.

Gas (9—Do not listen to idle gossip)
To dream of gas indicates you should beware of fire.

Gasoline (9—A trip for you)
To dream you buy gasoline is a warning that you should be saving with your money. To dream you run out of gasoline indicates delay, loss of money.

Gate (6—Go in and win)
To dream you enter a beautiful, wide gate indicates that a change is coming into your life. To find a closed gate indicates a large obstacle to surmount.

Geography (3—You will buy property)
To dream of geography indicates a coming trip.

Ghost (6—Spiritual help offered)
To dream of a ghost indicates that, chances are, your soul really encountered one.

Gift (6—A good dream)
To dream you receive a beautiful gift is a premonition you will receive one soon.

Glass (4—Secrets disclosed)

To dream of glass indicates a smooth life ahead.

Gloves (8—Take care in business dealings)

To buy, sell, or wear gloves indicates you will meet an underhanded stranger in the very near future. Beware!

Glue (9—Your friends will be loyal)

To dream of glue in any way indicates that you are capable of controlling many things at one time.

Goat (7—A good dream)

To dream of a god indicates good luck, health, and long life.

Gold (2—A good dream)

To dream of gold indicates that work, pleasure, travel, and gain are in store for you very soon.

Golf (4—You will visit the country)

To dream of golfing indicates you should not waste your energies on vain pursuits.

Gopher (6—Care is needed in work or home)

To dream you see or are bothered by gophers indicates someone is trying to undermine your position or business.

Graduate (5—A new door opens for you)

To dream that you graduate from some school of learning indicates a new position in life for you.

Grandparents (9—Help from friends or relatives)

To dream of your grandparents indicates love from the opposite sex.

Grapes (3—Liquor will be given, a present)

To dream of a grape arbor or fields of grapes indicates unlooked for prosperity. This is a good dream.

Grass (1—A very good dream)

To dream of flourishing, well-kept grass indicates nearness and refinement, and also prosperity in the near future. Dead grass indicates wasted worldly goods. Green grass is a good dream.

Grasshopper (7—You will have a garden; watch it)

To dream of grasshoppers means that a plague will sweep the country.

Grave (8—Tears over the past; don't lament)

To dream of an open grave indicates a death in your family soon. A closed grave means there will be no death near you for a long time.

Grindstone (8—Follow your next hunch)

To dream of a grindstone indicates you should sharpen your intuition; grasp troubles firmly and they will turn into money; be positive in your convictions and firm in your demands. To dream of sharpening knives on a grindstone indicates a new opportunity. If you succeed in putting a good edge on the knife, you will have success in this new undertaking.

Grocery (1—You will go shopping)

To dream of a grocery indicates that many opportunities are coming your way—big and little. There will be so many, be careful you select the right one.

Guitar (4—A harmonious home)

For a single person to dream of a guitar indicates coming love and marriage; for a married person, harmony in the home.

Gum (5—Avoid others' trouble)

To dream you are chewing gum is an indication that you should not repeat something you hear. If this gum is smeared on you, you will get into trouble if you do repeat what you hear.

Gun (6—A past incident bothers you)

To dream of a gun and that someone is trying to shoot you indicates that you should beware of an enemy.

Gypsy (2—Be careful of a loss)

To dream of a gypsy indicates you will take a trip into primitive country. Be careful that you do not lose your way on this trip.

> Come to me in my dreams, and then
> By day I shall be well again,
> For then the night will more than pay
> The hopeless longing of the day.
>
> Matthew Arnold

▾ H ▾

Hail (See Snow)

Hair (9—A visit to the barber or beauty parlor)
To dream that you are brushing and have beautiful hair indicates you should entertain bright hopes for the future. To have thin, ugly hair indicates you are not managing your affairs in the proper way.

Hall (6—A new home)
To dream of a large hall and you enter same indicates a mammoth opportunity is coming your way.

Hammock (1—Comfort through right decision)
To dream you are lying in a hammock in the cool shade indicates a wedding among your close friends.

Hand (9—You will receive some jewelry)
To dream your hands are beautiful and white indicates a present from someone to adorn them. If they are ugly and red, it means sickness.

Handkerchief (5—You will buy linen)
If a single person, this dream means flirtation; if married, new friends.

Happy (3—Laughter is good for the soul)
To dream you are happy indicates you really will be very happy.

Hardware (6—New cooking utensils or tools)
To dream of hardware or a hardware store indicates plenty of hard work in store for you.

Harem (9—You will have many admirers)
To dream of a harem indicates that your soul really did peek in on one while you slept.

Harvest (3—A good dream)
To dream of harvesting a large crop indicates wealth. A poor crop means poverty.

Hat (2—Do not be vain)
To dream of buying a new hat indicates new knowledge.

Hate (7—No one is big enough to hate)
To dream you hate a person indicates that that person hates you.

Hay (7—Abundance coming)

To dream of fields of uncut hay, grain, or clover indicates a great inheritance or great wealth in the future. Baled hay means that great wealth in stocks or bonds will be inherited. Hay or grain in any form is a good dream.

Health (6—Remember we are all perfect)

To dream you have good health indicates you will have good health in the future.

Hearse (See Funeral)

Heart (7—Someone will bare their heart to you)

To dream of heartache or of a pain in the heart indicates that there is a depressing condition about you, and you should get to work and eliminate it.

Heaven (1—A wonderful dream)

To dream of heaven indicates that you may have visited there while you were asleep.

Hedge (2—Private affairs will turn out well)

To dream of a hedge indicates you should keep your private affairs to yourself, as someone may try to pry into them.

Hell (1—Choose new friends carefully)

To dream of Hell, since there is no such place, indicates you should not be led by foolish fancies. Pay no attention to the flattery of a new friend or admirer.

Hermit (1—Take up a hobby)

To dream of a hermit indicates you should cultivate friends so you will not be lonely.

Hives (9—A troublesome issue is settled)

To dream you have hives indicates that lies will be told about you.

Hog (3—Money)

To dream of hogs indicates plenty.

Home (5—You will improve your surroundings)

To dream of home or of the home folks is a good omen.

Homesick (2—Do not lament over the past)

To dream of being homesick means that there is in your heart a longing for days that are past which cannot be gratified.

Horn (1—Go out and win, circulate)

To dream of playing a horn or any other kind of wind instrument indicates that you will become popular and gain a better position in life if you will be more aggressive.

Hornet (8—Angry words; be careful)

To dream of a hornet means you should look out for danger.

Horoscope (See Astrology)

Horse (2—Good luck)

The horse represents faithful friends. To dream of riding a horse indicates good health. To buy a horse indicates a new friend or a new love affair. To sell a horse or see a sick horse indicates the loss of a friend. To steal a horse is a warning against ill-gotten gains. To drive one means honor in the near future. A field full of horses, all fat and full of life, indicates that many new, influential friends are in store for you. To enter a barn full of horses indicates that you will start a new business enterprise, or that a new position will be offered you, or a raise of pay. To dream of a riding master indicates you should watch out for a domineering person. Plowing with a horse indicates hard work and good money in store for you within three months. Driving a team hitched to a wagon indicates slow but lasting prosperity. To curry a horse indicates that you will help a friend. A curry comb is a sign of hard work ahead. Ponies indicate new babies in the family circle. A mule indicates that a constant friend will help you in need. Beautiful harness, bridles, and saddles indicate that the dreamer will purchase new clothes through the help of a friend. To dream of a horse trader warns you against a deceitful friend.

Hospital (1—Take care of your health)

To dream of a hospital in any way indicates a sick spell.

Howl (4—A death in the neighborhood)

To dream you hear a dog howl or any other animal indicates loneliness in your life.

Hungry (3—Eat and meditate)

To dream you are hungry indicates you truly are.

Hunting (3—Not a good dream)

To dream of hunting indicates want.

Hurricane (See Wind)

Husband (6—If married, buy nice things to please him)

To dream of your husband indicates he has your welfare at heart. To dream he is not true indicates you both have enemies.

Dreams are true while they last, and do we not live in dreams?

Alfred Lord Tennyson

▾ I ▾

Ice, Icicles (See Snow)

Ice Cream (3—A banquet)

To dream of eating ice cream indicates coming good times.

Implore (4—Listen to a good friend)

To dream you implore someone for something you want or something you want them to do indicates your desires are not best for you in your waking hours.

Incense (6—A prayer is needed)

To dream of smelling or burning incense indicates a blessing and future happiness. This is a good dream.

Incline (3—Crowning success is coming)

To dream you go up a long incline indicates that much tedious work is in store for you, but it will be crowned with success. To go down an incline indicates you should go slowly in whatever you do and guide your affairs well.

Indian (6—A spiritual guidance given)

To dream of an Indian of any kind indicates you have a guiding spirit. Try to cultivate this Indian's friendship in thought.

Inheritance (See Money)

Ink (7—You will sign a legal paper)

To dream of using ink in writing indicates that something you do will have a lasting memory.

Insects (8—Constant money, small allowance)

To dream of insects of any kind indicates small gains and small worries.

Instruct (7—Your help will be needed)

To dream of instructing someone or many indicates you should develop some talent you have. Also you have some knowledge that you could impart to others that would benefit them.

Insurance (5—Security in old age)

To dream you have insurance or about insurance indicates you will be protected by loving friends in time of need. Also indicates you should not worry about anything, for you are spiritually protected.

Interpret, Interpreter (8—Gossip)

To dream you take an introduction or give one indicates you will make new friends in the spirit world, also new friends in your waking hours.

Invent (3—Go in and win; luck ahead)

To dream you invent something or are interested in inventions means you should cultivate the thought along this line. There is something you should invent, for this dream is trying to convey it to you.

Invitation (7—A wedding)

To dream you have an invitation indicates you will receive an invitation. This is a good dream.

Ironing (5—Work, pleasure, and money)

To dream of ironing indicates that you will straighten out your affairs and your difficulties to your satisfaction.

Island (5—You will buy or sell land)

To dream you are on a beautiful island indicates you will possess something in life, a lovely home or estate. Also indicates lonely days ahead for you.

Ivory (7—A good dream)

To dream of ivory in any form indicates you will leave a lasting memory here on earth of some achievement that you do while here. Also indicates you have to combat stubborn thoughts of old people. Ivory also indicates long life.

> *In blissful dream, in silent night,*
> *There came to me, with magic might,*
> *With magic might, my own sweet love,*
> *Into my little room above.*

Heinrich Heine

▾ J ▾

Jail (5—Nagging friends or relatives)
To dream of a jail or you are in jail indicates a nagging condition around you. Also you are not permitted to expand and do the things you want. Jail indicates the retarding of progress. Concentrate to overcome this condition. Jail is not a good dream.

Jewels (2—A good dream)
To dream of precious jewels is a very good omen. If you dream of gold jewelry, it indicates kindness, purity of heart, and good deeds. If you dream of possessing diamonds, it means you will have a very brilliant future. Precious stones indicates that time is precious, so you must use it to good advantage. To be given a beautiful ring indicates eternal friendship and love from someone. To lose your jewels indicates your time is wasted and the loss of friends. As jewels always represent time, and also precious stones of any kind, to dream of these is always an indication that you should spend your time well and learn something to your advantage.

Joke (9—Fun but expensive)
To dream of playing a joke or having a joke played on you indicates you will find out something you dislike.

Journey (9—Concentrate on your problem)
To dream of a journey indicates an upset condition of your mind. It also means you are trying to make a decision on an important matter. If the journey is pleasant, the decision will turn out right. If the journey is unpleasant, it indicates you should concentrate to make the right decision.

July (5—If married, new dishes and table set)

To dream of the month of July indicates social activities and good times in store.

Jump (6—Practice cultural actions; it pays)

To dream you are jumping or people are jumping around indicates you should be more dignified and use poise to gain success.

Jury (2—Disregard others' advice; use your own)

To dream of a jury indicates that much criticism is coming your way. Use your own good judgment and pay no attention to this criticism.

It is the fault of dreamers to fear fate.

Stephen Phillips

▾ **K** ▾

Kangaroo (1—Slow down, relax)

To dream of a kangaroo is a warning against leaping before you look. Do not make hasty decisions.

Kettle (1—A better home with contentment)

To dream of a boiling kettle indicates a change of affairs for you.

Key (5—A new offer soon)

To dream of a key indicates you will be taken into a new business, something you will go into with the help of friends. This is a good dream.

Kill (9—The end of a disagreeable condition)

To dream you see something killed or to dream you kill something indicates the loss of something, the end of something, which happens very abruptly. If you kill something that attacks you, you will overcome your enemies. To kill something accidentally means loss and worry through neglect on your part.

King (5—You will meet a famous person)

To dream of a king in any way indicates that high honors will be bestowed upon you. This is a very good dream.

Kiss (4—Friendship; help when needed)

To dream you are kissed means warm friendship and help when it is needed. To have a woman bestow a kiss on a woman indicates deceit. To be kissed by your sweetheart, if single, means a coming engagement.

Kitchen (7—You will remodel a house)

To dream of a beautiful kitchen indicates a new home.

Kite (9—Unlooked for opportunity soon)

To dream of a kite indicates high ideals which you should cultivate, as they will carry you to success.

Knock (9—A spiritual message awaits you)

To dream you hear someone knock on your door indicates someone wants to call on you. To hear a knock of any kind indicates news is coming.

> Some must delve when the dawn is nigh;
> Some must toil when the noonday beams;
> But when the night comes, and the soft winds sigh,
> Every man is a King of Dreams.

Clinton Scollard

▾ L ▾

Laboratory (1—You will hear of a great discovery)

To dream of a well-equipped laboratory indicates you should follow a pursuit along this line.

Lace (3—A wonderful dream)

To dream of beautiful hand-made lace indicates you should follow a pursuit along this line. It also indicates beautiful lasting deeds that will endear you to your friends long after you have gone. This is a good dream.

Ladder (8—If you own a home, you will paint it)

To dream you climb a ladder indicates that you should be sure you want what you are after, for fields look very green from a distance. To go down a ladder means disappointment.

Lamp (6—A guiding light to help you)

To dream you light a lamp indicates a sudden enlightenment on some subject or work you are doing, which will please you very much.

Lane (5—A good dream)

To dream you stroll in a beautiful lane indicates a better condition in your life in the future. If this is a long lane, you will prosper more as time goes along.

Late (2—Do not waste your time)

To dream you are late and your time is limited and your clothes just won't go on while you dress, and when you do succeed in getting dressed, you miss your car, all this indicates you are retarded by others, for you would be successful if you could do as you wish.

Laugh (4—Tears)

To dream you laugh or hear someone laughing indicates insincerity of friends.

Lawsuit (6—You may be called as a witness)

If you dream of being sued, beware of envy or trickery on the part of the one suing. If you are suing, be careful to be just and upright in your dealings.

Lawyer (3—A legal paper to sign)

To dream of a lawyer or judge indicates you will hear an argument pro and con by two people, also a friend talked about and befriended.

Letters (9—Hasty news soon)

To dream of letters indicates you really will receive a letter. To write one means someone is longing to hear from you. Hasty news indicates news of a wedding, birth, or death. Letters of any kind indicate news.

Library (4—You will buy a picture)

To dream of a library indicates knowledge; you will learn something in the near future which will be to your advantage.

License (4—You will give charity)

To dream of buying a license of any kind indicates waste of money and servitude. Take care after such a dream.

Lies (9—Do not share in idle gossip)

To dream someone lies to you or about you indicates that this generally is true. If you recognize the guilty party, be careful in their company and avoid associating with them at all.

Lightship (9—Be careful if you fly or sail)

To dream of a lightship warns you to be very cautious in your waking hours, for danger is ahead.

Linen (9—A good dream)

To dream of beautiful linens indicates that plenty is in store for you, comfort and a good home.

Liquor (2—You will attend a party)

To dream of liquor indicates plenty and squandered money.

Load (5—A good dream)

To dream of carrying a load of any kind indicates illness. A truckload or carload of provisions or of anything useful indicates plenty.

Lodge (7—An invitation to join one soon)

To dream of a lodge or an order of some kind indicates that hidden secrets will be discovered.

Lonely (2—Make new friends)

To dream you are lonely indicates sadness.

Loom (See Weaving)

Lose (6—Cheer up; better days are ahead)

To dream you lose your way indicates a troubled mental condition. To dream you lose an address where you live or where you are going indicates you will lose out in some new undertaking. There is a retarding here of some kind.

Love (9—If single, a proposal)

To dream that others love you indicates that they really do.

Luck (2—Think good luck; it will come)

To dream you have good luck means you really will have. To dream you have bad luck indicates you should change your way of thinking.

Lumber (8—Work you like)

To dream of lumber or a lumberyard indicates a new home. If you are a working person, there is much work in store for you. To dream of cutting lumber indicates you should form well-made plans. Lumber, on the whole, is a lucky dream.

Luxury (See Abundance)

I arise from dreams of thee
In the first sweet sleep of night,
When the winds are breathing low,
And the stars are shining bright.

Percy Bysshe Shelley

▾ M ▾

Machine (8—A new job or business for you)

To dream of a machine or machinery of any kind indicates fast progress to future success.

Madonna (8—Give thanks in prayer)

To dream of a Madonna indicates refinement, kindness, and loving thoughts bestowed upon you by others. This is a good dream.

Magic (6—Do not hide your talents)

To dream of magic or magicians indicates you will discover that someone is trying to cheat you. If you enjoy the magic, it indicates unlooked for gains.

Magnifying Glass (1—A good dream)

To dream of a magnifying glass indicates plenty. Your plans for the future will turn out better than you expected.

Manikin (8—Kindness pays)

To dream of a manikin or an artist's model indicates that you are either following a vain pursuit or a vain person around annoys you. Also indicates you are in need of sympathy.

Mantilla (1—You will attend a fiesta)

To dream of a beautiful mantilla indicates refinement, culture, and pleasant days ahead.

Manufacturing (3—If in business, new ideas pay)

To dream of manufacturing anything indicates an unstable disposition. To dream of success in manufacturing indicates a change of position.

Manuscript (8—Someone is awaiting a letter; write)

To dream of a manuscript indicates that to succeed you will have to work hard.

Marble (6—A beautiful home and income)

To dream of the month of March indicates a great change coming in your life.

Market (5—New things for the home will be bought)

To dream of a well-stocked market indicates that a plentiful supply will be yours as you grow older. To dream of a poorly stocked market indicates want in the future.

Marriage (See Wedding)

Mask (8—You will uncover deceit)

To dream you wear a mask indicates you should not try to deceive anyone, for your actions will be detected. To dream someone else wears a mask means you will soon discover someone is trying to deceive you or hide something from you.

Match (9—Do not quarrel)

To dream of matches, if single, indicates a passing fancy; if married, a quarrel with your mate.

Mausoleum (See Funeral)

May (3—A potted plant will be given to you)

To dream of the month of May, if single, indicates a proposal.

Meadow (See Grass)

Measure (1—Do not cheat yourself)

To dream of measuring something indicates someone will be very exacting with you.

Meat (3—Health, wealth, and happiness)

To dream of meat of any kind represents strength.

Medal (8—Popularity and fame in store)

To dream you receive a medal, or are decorated with great pomp and splendor, as this is a good dream, indicates that you will receive a high honor.

Medicine (See Drugs)

Melon (5—You will buy stocks or bonds)

To dream you cut or eat a big, juicy, ripe melon on a hot day indicates prosperity. If the melon is green, or if you have only a small portion, an investment will turn out to be no good.

Metal (6—A good dream)

To dream of gold indicates wealth and purity of heart. Ore indicates that opportunities will be presented to you in a crude state. All metals represent good things in some form. Also metals are a good dream. To dream of mining metals indicates an inheritance.

Message (See News, Telephone)

Milk, Milking (9—A christening)

To dream of milk or milking indicates good health and an addition to the family circle. To one in the dairy business it indicates many new customers.

Mill, Miller (1—Detailed work in store)

To dream of a mill or miller indicates that you will display a finesse in your chosen work which will bring you success and recognition. If you are a manufacturer, your product will be in demand. To dream of a miller or miller indicates refinement.

Minister (9—Prayer is needed)

To dream of a minister indicates you will be reprimanded for something that you do.

Miser (1—Buy what you need)

To dream of a miser is a warning against thinking in a small, petty way, for if you do, you will bring poverty upon yourself.

Mistletoe (1—Happiness ahead)

To dream of being kissed under the mistletoe, if single, indicates a proposal; if married, a flirtation.

Money (9—A good dream)

To dream you possess a large amount of money indicates that you will possess it if you hold the right thought toward it. To find money indicates loss and disappointment. Money, on the whole, is a good dream.

After such a dream, think progressive, prosperous thoughts. Follow your intuition.

Moon (3—If single, a new admirer)

To dream of the moon in any way indicates you will have love bestowed upon you in your darkest hours.

Mortgage (7—A new lease on life soon)

To dream that you buy, sell, or execute a mortgage indicates worry, loss, and debt. To dream of paying a mortgage indicates release from obligation or the happy solution of an annoying condition.

Mosquito (3—Ungrateful relatives or friends)

To dream of mosquitoes indicates that you will be bothered by borrowers who will never repay their obligations to you.

Moth (2—Be careful of cigarettes)

To dream of moths indicates loss of clothing or bed clothing by fire. This is not a good dream.

Mother (7—A blessing from her)

To dream of your mother, whether she is dead or alive, indicates that you have communed with her.

Mountain (8—A wonderful dream)

To dream you are in some vast mountains indicates you will accomplish some very big things in life. A very deep canyon means you should take care in what you do. A big cliff protruding from the side of a mountain indicates danger. To dream you climb a mountain indicates that through hard work a very high position in life is awaiting you. To dream of mountains is a very good dream.

Mouse, Mousetrap (1—Beware of a thief)

To dream of a mouse indicates that there are those who are envious of your possessions or talents. To dream of catching a mouse in a trap indicates that you thwart an enemy.

Moving (8—A new life)

To dream you are moving indicates that a dissatisfied condition exists in your surroundings. To dream you are packing and preparing to move indicates you will overcome this condition. Moving indicates a change of some kind in your life.

Mud (4—A hard fight, but you will win)

To dream of mud indicates that you will have to wade over and through many people in order to succeed.

Mule (6—Stubborn associates encountered)

To dream of a mule indicates that you will encounter an ignorant and stubborn person. Ignore such a person.

Museum (See Antiques, Art Gallery)

Music (2—A good dream)

To dream you hear beautiful music means you truly do. To dream that you are endeavoring to play any kind of instrument or you hear someone trying to play an instrument indicates that there will be many people in tune with your efforts. Music and musical instruments of any kind is a very good dream.

Mustache (9—Dress well; it pays)

To dream you have a mustache is a warning against becoming slovenly in your habits.

> *I had a dream which was not at all a dream.*
>
> Lord Byron

▾ N ▾

Nail (9—Be careful of a sharp object)

To dream of a nail of any kind, fingernail or iron nail, indicates you will discover the truth of something that has been worrying you.

Naked (8—Beware of borrowers)

To dream you are stripped of your clothing indicates a jealous person will defame your character and your name. You will have much petty jealousy to combat.

Navy (8—Talks of war)

To dream of the navy or someone connected with the navy indicates rumors of war.

Necklace (6—Do not make hasty promises)

To dream of wearing or receiving a necklace indicates a vow which must be fulfilled.

Needle (9—You will hear sharp words)

To dream of needles indicates people will pry into your affairs. To sew with a needle indicates you will successfully evade them. Any pointed thing, like a pin or needle, indicates meddling and worry.

Negro (5—You will hear good music)

To dream of Negroes means harmony in the things you do.

Neighbor (6—Flowers will be given to you)

Nest (See Eggs)

News (7—Important news on the radio)

To dream of hearing or reading important news is a forerunner of news to come.

New Year's Day (5—A new beginning soon)

This dream indicates a new start in life; if you are happy, prosperity. This is a good dream.

Numbers (2—A good dream)

To see numbers in a dream indicates good luck.

Nun (4—Loneliness)

To dream of a nun indicates sadness.

Nurse (5—You will visit the sick)

To dream of a nurse indicates good health. To dream of nursing someone indicates sickness.

Nuts (2—An unexpected package arrives)

To dream of nuts of any kind indicates the secret support of your endeavor without your knowledge. To dream of nuts of any kind is a very good dream.

Meet me in Dreamland, sweet dreamy Dreamland,
There let my dreams come true.

Beth Slater Whitson

▾ **O** ▾

Ocean (2—A good dream)

To dream of the ocean means you are of a restless nature and you should cultivate a more serene nature to succeed. To dream you sail on the ocean is a very good dream, as it foretells that some of your dreams will come true. To travel on a large oceanliner means that some great desire you have will be fulfilled. To dream of boating means slow progress, especially if you have to row the boat. To skip along over the water in a motor-driven boat means fast progress. To dream of a clear lake of water is a very good dream. Water means life. If you dream you are by a peaceful lake, your life should be very serene for some years to come, especially if there are many trees and grass nearby. To dream of a clear river means that through life you will never want, but you will have to travel some rough places to succeed. To dream of muddy or dirty water means to be careful you do not do something to dirty your name.

October (6—A good dream)

To dream of the month of October indicates a picnic in the country.

Officer (8—If you drive, look out for a ticket)

To dream of an officer of the law indicates trouble.

Olives (1—Unlooked for riches)

To dream of olives indicates plenty.

Oil, Oil Field (See Derrick)

Orchestra (See Music)

Orient (9—A mysterious visitor)

To dream of the Orient indicates you will solve an unsolved mystery.

Orphan (9—Someone needs your sympathy)

To dream of an orphan indicates loneliness.

Ostrich (See Birds)

Owl (See Birds)

Oyster (See Fish, Food)

> *In dreams doth he behold her*
> *Still fair and kind and young.*
>
> Andrew Lang

▾ P ▾

Package (See Box)

Paint, Painting (6—A good dream)
To dream of painting anything indicates a big change coming into your life. The more you paint, or have painted, the bigger the change. This is a good dream.

Pall Bearer (See Funeral)

Palmistry (7—You will find out the true facts)
To dream of having your palm read indicates a long life.

Parade (9—You will chat, laugh, and dance)
To dream of witnessing a parade indicates an invitation to some place of amusement.

Paralysis (3—Do not complain)
To dream of paralysis indicates frustration in your efforts. You can overcome this by concentration.

Pardon (See Convict)

Park (See Grass)

Parrot (7—Do not believe all you hear)
To dream of a parrot indicates that you will be annoyed by a person who talks too much. It is also a warning for you to bridle your own tongue.

Parting (4—A new door opens for you)
To dream of parting indicates tears.

Partner, Partnership (2—Beware of waste)
To dream of a partner or partnership is not a good dream. Take good care of your finances in the future.

Passenger (5—You will be asked for a loan)
To dream you carry a passenger indicates that you will be annoyed by spongers.

Passport (7—Be careful of valuable papers)
Trouble over a passport indicates coming trouble over papers of some kind, possibly loss of papers.

Pastry (8—Do not waste food)

To dream of eating pastry indicates waste.

Pawnshop (4—Not a good dream)

This dream indicates want and waste. This is not a good dream. To buy something at a pawn shop indicates gain.

Peaches (See Fruit)

Pearls (See Jewels)

Pears (See Fruit)

Pelican (See Birds)

Pen, Pencil (8—Answer your letters promptly)

A dream of pen or pencil indicates news; also a gift from a distance.

Perfume (See Aroma)

Photography (See Camera, Art Gallery)

Physician (See Doctor)

Picnic (See Entertainment)

Pig (See Hog)

Pigeon (See Birds)

Pillow (See Bed)

Pimple (See Boils)

Pineapple (See Fruit)

Plow (See Horse)

Police (See Officer)

Potato (See Vegetables)

Practice (8—Added pleasures)

Prairie (3—Everything will be better for you)

To dream of a prairie indicates a great expansion in your outlook on your life and work.

Prayer (1—A wonderful dream)

Pregnancy (See Baby)

Priest (See Minister)

Print (5—Strive hard to please others)

To dream of printing or typing anything indicates you will do something to leave a lasting impression here. This is a good dream.

Prize (2—Radio announcement soon on prizes)

To dream you win a prize indicates there is much happiness in store for you.

Prize Fight, Prize Fighters (7—Not a good dream)

To dream of attending a prize fight, a bull fight, or a cock fight indicates that you will be subjected to brutal treatment at the hands of ignorant people. For a fighter to dream of winning a fight indicates that he will lose. As fighting is such an unnecessary evil, this is a bad dream.

Program (7—You will hear a famous person speak)

To dream of a program or that you are reading one indicates that many changes of all kinds will be in your life. Each change will be for the better.

Property (7—Buy property)

To dream you own much property indicates many worries; also coming wealth. On the whole, this is a good dream.

Propose (5—New business deal soon)

To dream someone proposes to you, if you are single, means you really will be proposed to. To others, a business proposition will be offered.

Prowler (8—Guard your purse)

To dream you hear a prowler on your premises indicates people are snooping into your affairs. Be on your guard after this dream.

Pump (3—Steady income indicated)

To dream you pump at an old-fashioned well indicates that hard work is in store for you. To see an electric pump at work indicates you will profit by someone else's labor or efforts.

Purchase (2—A good dream)

To dream you are shopping or buying real estate or anything in large quantities indicates you will make well-laid plans for the future. This dream indicates expansion of some kind.

Purse (7—Money coming unexpected)

To dream you lose your purse indicates a lost opportunity that would have been very profitable for you. To find another's purse indicates an opportunity will be offered and it will be profitable if you accept it. To return a purse to its rightful owner indicates you will share your profits with others.

Puzzle (7—Study is needed; read good books)

To dream you are working a puzzle or something puzzles you indicates it is a warning you are wasting valuable time.

Pyramid (5—Listen to a friend's advice)

To dream of the Pyramids indicates you should avoid frivolous endeavors and take up more stable and lasting endeavors.

> *Is this a dream? Oh, if it be a dream, let me sleep on,*
> *And do not wake me yet!*

Henry Wadsworth Longfellow

▾ Q ▾

Quarantine (3—Be more receptive to others' opinions)

To dream you are in quarantine indicates you are holding a limited thought around you. Concentrate on this, as expansion is needed.

Queen (8—A good dream)

To dream of a queen is a very good dream.

Quicksilver (1—Take your time on a decision)

This dream indicates quick wealth; also that you should exercise care in conserving it. As this dream represents haste, it is a good dream.

Quilting (1—You will purchase bedding)

To dream you are quilting indicates that through hard work and efficiency your future will be very successful. To dream of a quilt indicates you will profit through others.

> *In thoughts from the visions of the night, when deep sleep*
> *falleth on men.*

Job, iv, 13

▾ R ▾

Rabbit (7—A child will visit you)

To dream of rabbits indicates plentiful food.

Race (9—Be progressive)

To dream you attend the races or take part in a race indicates you should be constant in your endeavor in order to win in what you are doing. It is an indication you should keep up with the times in all things.

Radio (2—Spiritual guidance)

To dream you listen to a radio indicates a still voice will impart a message that will be of benefit to you.

Raffle (3—A lucky gamble; go and win)

To dream of a raffle or you win at a raffle indicates you will take some chances in business in the future.

Railroad (See Travel)

Rain (6—A good dream)

To dream it is raining indicates the termination of some unpleasant affair in your life. After this rain, if you see a beautiful rainbow in the sky, it indicates you truly will find a pot of gold at the end of the rainbow. To dream of dew, fog, or mist indicates that a clearing condition will come into your life. A hard storm with lightning and thunder indicates that true darkness will come into your life before the dawning of this new era, but after the rain the sun will shine again for you. This is a good dream, for a good change is indicated.

Rake (8—You will clean out old clothing)

To dream of raking leaves or grass indicates thrift and prosperity.

Ransom (See Money)

Recite (6—Others need your advice)

To dream that you are called upon to recite or make a speech indicates that your opinion is very much valued among your friends.

Regret (1—Forget the past; look to the future)

To dream you regret something you have done indicates sadness.

Rejuvenate (7—A good dream)

To dream you have your face or body rejuvenated in any way indicates added strength and vitality—good health.

Repair (4—Thrifty times ahead)

To dream you are repairing, mending, or beautifying anything indicates coming prosperity.

Rescue (6—You will be called upon to help)

To dream of rescuing another indicates a birth in the family.

Residence (1—A good dream)

To dream you build or buy a beautiful home indicates this is a very good dream. To dream of anything pertaining to the home—lovely furniture, etc.—means future prosperity, contentment. To dream you are losing your home indicates a lax condition in your management of affairs.

Resign (2—Stick up for your rights)

To dream you resign your position indicates that you should remain where you are. To resign yourself to some annoying condition indicates a weakness in your character that should not be tolerated.

Resort (5—A vacation soon, or trip)

To dream you take a vacation at a lovely summer resort indicates a new romance for single people and good times for married folks.

Rest (You should relax and read)

To dream you are resting means you really are.

Revenge (4—Give good for evil; it will pay)

To dream you revenge or are revenged indicates this is not a good dream. You truly have enemies.

Rice (8—Constant income)

Rice indicates plenty from many sources.

Rival (8—An unsettled condition)

To dream you have a rival indicates you should do a little investigation to see if you really have. This is not a good dream.

Road (2—New adventure)

To dream you travel over a big, wide road indicates plenty is in store for you and it will be easy for you to get. A rough road indicates you will succeed, but only by the sweat of your brow.

Roof (9—Lay up money for a rainy day)
To dream you have a good roof on your home indicates good fortune protects you. A leaky roof means your affairs are not well planned.

Rope (9—Good help from others when needed)
To dream of rope indicates robust health.

Rose, Rosebush (See Flower)

Rubber (5—Be pliable in your opinions)
To dream of rubber indicates a tendency to be too yielding for your own good. Stand up for your own rights. This dream also indicates an inheritance.

Ruins (9—Try harder; you will succeed)
To dream of seeing ruins indicates trials, tribulations, and waste. This dream is a warning that you should guard against drifting into a lax and shiftless attitude toward life.

Running (7—Smile and forget yesterday)
To dream of running away or trying to hide from a person or thing indicates that an unsatisfactory condition in your past life still reaches you with its vibration. You should disregard this dream and try to forget the past.

Rupture (2—Be careful)
To dream you have a rupture is a warning to guard against injuring yourself.

> *If I may trust the flattering truth of sleep,*
> *My dreams presage some joyful news at hand.*

William Shakespeare

▾ S ▾

Saddle (See Horse)

Sailing, Sailboat (See Water)

Sailor (2—Clouds of war)

To dream of a sailor or a soldier indicates protection from loved ones in time of need.

Saint (9—Pray for what you want)

To dream of a saint and you know which saint, it indicates he will grant your favor if you ask it of him.

Sale (1—You will be very busy)

To dream of a sale or you are selling things indicates profit and a busy time ahead for you.

Salt (7—Your opinion will be sought)

To dream of salt indicates good health.

Samples (4—You will buy many small purchases)

To dream of samples indicates a shopping trip to purchase small articles; also a gift.

Sand (See Desert)

Saw (7—A change is needed)

A saw indicates the loss of a friend or the severing of diplomatic relations.

Scales (5—Justice for a wrong deed)

To dream of scales indicates you should show justice and mercy to those dependent upon you. If you have a lawsuit, it will be decided in your favor. This is a good dream.

Scandal (9—If a professional person, a new contract)

To dream of scandal indicates that you will acquire fame or that you will meet a famous person.

Scarab (8—Good luck in store for you)

To dream you see a scarab or possess one indicates long life.

Scrapbook (1—Good days to come)

To dream of a scrapbook indicates that you will talk over the good times of the past with a friend.

Scythe (8—You will divide with a relative)

A scythe indicates a new start in life coming soon.

Seaport (See Water)

Seed (6—A new job or business soon)
To dream you are planting seed or planting anything indicates that from your endeavors you will reap a good harvest. This is a good dream.

Sermon (3—Your prayers will be answered)
To dream you hear a good sermon at church indicates you will be inspired to great accomplishments.

Servant (9—You will be called upon to help others)
To dream of a servant or help in any capacity indicates that through others you will succeed. After this dream, be loyal, just, and accommodating to people around you and your fellow workers.

Sewing (5—A good dream)
To dream of making new clothing indicates new clothes for the sewer. To dream of patching old clothes indicates that you try too hard to economize. There is plenty here, and you should reach out for your share. Making a beautiful quilt indicates prosperity. Scissors indicate sharp bargains, especially if the scissors are very sharp. Needles and thimbles indicate help from friends. Sewing, on the whole, is a very nice dream.

Shade (1—Kindness shown from friends)
To dream you stop in the shade of a beautiful tree indicates you will meet a friend whose company is very refreshing to you.

Shake Hands (9—A greeting awaits you)
When you dream you shake hands with a person, whether living or dead, this is not really a dream but is an actual gesture—your spirit is making contact with the person while your body sleeps.

Sheep, Shepherd (See Animals)

Shell (2—A present)
To dream of shells means wasted time.

Ship, Shipping (See Water)

Shoes, Shoemaker (3—A good dream)
To dream of new shoes indicates a trip by water. To dream of a shoemaker indicates that you will meet a very fine traveling companion. Any kind of footwear indicates travel.

Shooting (See Gun)

Shovel (9—Money through work)

To shovel clean earth means prosperity. To clean up dirt and rubbish with a shovel indicates coming wealth. The more you shovel, the greater the wealth.

Silk (6—You will buy new clothing)

To dream of silk or silkworms indicates spiritual blessing. This dream is a good omen.

Silver, Silverware (4—A good dream)

If a young woman dreams of silver, she will be married soon. For a married person to dream of beautiful silverware indicates an inheritance. To dream of mining silver indicates health and wealth. Silver or silver money is a good dream.

Sin (6—Keep yourself above approach)

To dream that you sin indicates you will be ashamed of something in your waking hours.

Sing (4—Tears and sadness)

To dream of singing indicates bad luck, sorrow, and tears.

Single (3—If married, company visits)

To dream of being single indicates loneliness.

Skate (2—A good dream)

To dream you skate in a lovely skating rink indicates that after great effort your life will run smoothly.

Skin (8—You will visit a barber or beauty parlor)

To dream your skin is beautiful indicates happiness. To dream your skin is rough, red, and pimpled indicates money, a change, and tears.

Slaughterhouse (7—Be careful in traffic)

This dream indicates a death, disappointment, or sadness. This is not a good dream.

Smoke (9—Go in and win)

To dream you smoke or you are around somebody who is smoking indicates you will conquer future obstacles by concentration. You will dream about doing many things, but through a lax condition on your part they will never develop.

Snake (5—Avoid drink; not good for you)

To dream of a snake does not mean an enemy, as most people think; it only means that you or someone about you has low desires. After this dream, choose your associates wisely and refrain from pastimes where morals are concerned that might ruin your health. Snakes indicate infection.

Snow (8—A wonderful dream)

To dream you awake in the morning and the ground is covered with beautiful white snow indicates that a wonderful change is coming into your life. To dream of frost and ice means a slight change in your life. Anything pertaining to cold weather is good.

Soap (6—A good dream)

To dream of soap in any form indicates passing fancies. Don't take petty worries too seriously.

Soldiers (4—Not a good dream)

To dream of soldiers indicates war.

Sowing (5—Plenty of action)

To dream of sowing means money going out and money coming in.

Spice (7—Perfume will be given)

To dream of any kind of spice or seasoning of any kind indicates a mixed fortune.

Spider (8—Annoying letters)

To dream of a spider indicates enemies, deceit, and entanglements, if you are not careful. This is a bad dream.

Spinster (8—You will plan a knitted dress)

To dream of an old maid indicates you will have to help an old relative.

Sponge (4—You will go fishing or near water)

To dream of a sponge indicates you may encounter inflated ego, either your own or someone else's.

Spur (2—If you ride, be careful)

To dream of a spur indicates you will witness some cruelty.

Spy (6—Be careful what you say or write)

To dream of a spy indicates someone is trying to pry into your affairs. Be on your guard.

Star (4—Fond hopes realized)

To dream of the stars indicates happy days are ahead for you.

Story (7—A spiritual help near)

To dream you hear a beautiful story indicates that some spirit really does tell you that story.

Strawberries (See Fruit)

Sugar (3—A friendly caller)

To dream of sugar indicates flattery from the opposite sex.

Suicide (See Funeral)

Sun (9—A new opportunity soon)

To dream the sun is shining brightly and it is a lovely day indicates coming prosperity. To dream of an eclipse of the sun means there will be a big change in your life, the passing of the old and the coming of the new.

Survey (2—Make well-laid plans)

To dream you are surveying indicates your plans will be laid and will materialize.

Swamp (9—You will discover a hidden asset)

To dream of a big, wild swamp indicates you will make a big discovery or perfect an invention.

Swan (See Birds)

Sweetheart (7—Love and happiness in store)

To dream of your sweetheart indicates happy days ahead.

Swimming (See Water)

Swing (9—Balance your judgment)

To dream you are swinging indicates you should be very constant in your endeavors.

Sympathy (9—A blessing)

To dream you sympathize with someone indicates your soul encountered someone who really needed sympathy, and you truly gave this sympathy while you were asleep. To dream someone gave you sympathy indicates somebody did sympathize with you.

And the King said unto them, I have dreamed a dream, and my spirit was troubled to know the dream.

Dan. ii, 3

▾ T ▾

Table (4—Plenty in store for you)

To dream of a beautifully set table, with lovely silverware and linen and dishes, indicates happiness is in store for you—company and entertainment. This is a good dream.

Tabloid (8—Bright entertainment soon)

To dream of a tabloid indicates a bright outlook in what you are doing. This is a good dream.

Talk (8—Beware of new acquaintance)

To dream you hear much talking and undertone indicates a trouble-maker is at work; be on your guard.

Tambourine (1—A beggarly gift received)

To dream of a tambourine indicates you will be approached by a beggar.

Tapestry (7—A good dream)

To dream of a beautiful tapestry indicates good fortune ahead.

Tattoo (1—Not a good dream)

To dream you see a tattoo or have one put on your body indicates you should be careful so as not to become involved in scandals that will harm you for the rest of your life.

Taxes (6—Poor bargains)

To dream of paying taxes indicates a waste of money.

Tea (8—Good health)

A dream about tea, tea cups, tea kettle, or anything pertaining to tea is a good dream. It indicates a pleasant social life in the future.

Teeth (4—Petty annoyances)

To dream your teeth hurt you or you lose them indicates you should see that they really do not pain you while you sleep before you take stock in this dream. To dream you visit a dentist means you will have new friends. To dream you lose the fillings or the caps off your teeth means disagreeable words. Teeth on the whole are petty worries. I never take much stock in such a dream. Teeth are so sensitive and so near the brain that they register every little thing there. Just disregard a dream about teeth.

Telephone (1—You will receive hasty news)

To dream you talk over the telephone with the dead or the living indicates they are trying to send a message through to you.

Tenant (2—You will meet a hateful person)

To dream of a tenant is not a good dream. It means disappointment or disillusionment.

Tent (5—A trip to the country, hunting)

To dream of a tent indicates coming hardships.

Theatre (5—A gay party)

To dream of a theatre in any capacity indicates that you should not spend your time with too many frivolous things.

Thief (3—Guard your purse)

To dream of a thief indicates you should beware of envious fair-weather friends or new acquaintances. To dream that you steal, or see others stealing, indicates you should beware of sickness or accident.

Thimble (See Sewing)

Thread (See Sewing)

Threshing (5—Riches through labor)

To dream of threshing indicates that you will collect a debt of long standing.

Thunder (See Rain)

Tobacco (5—Beware of fire)

To dream of tobacco in any form indicates that you should beware of reckless spending on frivolous objects.

Tomb (See Funeral)

Tools (9—A good dream)

To dream of any kind of tool indicates success will come to you through the clever way you use the tools that are put in your hands or the opportunities that come your way.

Tourist (See Travel)

Toys (7—A children's party soon)

This dream indicates pleasant pursuits, happiness, and a visit from a child.

Train (8—A good dream)

To dream you are traveling on a train indicates an upset mental condition, or that you are trying to make a decision which will eventually lead to a change of some kind.

Trap (1—A small theft)

To dream of any kind of a trap or that you trap something indicates that some kind of trick may be played on you or someone may try to cheat you.

Travel (6—A good dream)

To dream of planning a long trip indicates a great change in your life in the future—a move, a sale of property, buying a home, or some other vast change. Travel, on the whole, indicates a restlessness within. Sailing on a beautiful ship and reaching foreign soil indicates a new position or new business—a complete change in your occupation, a change for the better in your finances. In dreaming of shipping by water or any other way, large consignments of merchandise indicate profitable returns in the future from your endeavor. This is a good dream, as travel indicates change.

Treasure (8—Unexpected money)

To dream of a buried treasure indicates that someone's flattery may try to mislead you; be careful.

Tree (3—A good dream)

To dream of trees, soft wood, hardwood, or any kind of tree, indicates strength, good luck, prosperity, stability. Dead trees mean lost opportunities.

Trophy (3—A present soon)

To dream you win or see a beautiful trophy indicates you will achieve success, honor, or fame. This is a good dream.

Trousers (9—You will go shopping)

To dream of trousers indicates the purchase of two new articles of clothing.

Trunk (3—You will travel)

To dream of a trunk and lovely baggage indicates you will gather together opportunities and use them to your advantage. Lovely baggage in any form is a very good dream.

Tunnel (See Cave)

Turtle (See Animal)

Twin (3—Small annoyances)

To dream of a twin of anything indicates that a double portion of something is coming your way. This is a good dream.

Type, Typing, Typewriter (3—A good dream)

This dream indicates you should be careful about what you put into writing or about what you sign. It also indicates plenty of hard work in store, with much detail.

> *Is this a dream? Oh, if it be a dream, Let me sleep on.*
> *And do not wake me yet!*

Henry Wadsworth Longfellow

▾ U ▾

Umbrella (3—You will uncover deceit)

To dream of an umbrella indicates someone will try to cover up or hide some nice thing you have done and take the credit himself. Be on your guard after dreaming of a sunshade of any kind.

Umpire (1—Give kindly, fair advice)

To dream of an umpire means you will be called upon to settle a dispute. Keep out of this if you can.

Uniform (6—Indicates servitude)

To dream you see or wear beautiful uniforms indicates pride in something you are doing or an honor will be bestowed upon you.

Union (1—A business union to your advantage)

To dream you unite yourself with others indicates that as you grow older you will develop a very fine, strong character. This is a good dream.

> *"God came to Lahan, the Syrian, by night, in a dream, and said unto him, take heed that thou speak not to Jacob, either good or bad."*
>
> Gen. Xxxi, 24.

▾ V ▾

Vacant (7—Look for a new home)

To dream you walk through a vacant house or building indicates that you are not grasping opportunities and you are just marking time. Also indicates a dissatisfied condition exists. Try to overcome it.

Vaccinate (6—Look at the label, then purchase)

To dream of being vaccinated indicates that you will receive a gift which you do not care for.

Valentine (3—A loving thought sent to you)

To dream of this beautiful love token indicates love and esteem and happiness. An ugly valentine means an insult.

Vase (See Art Gallery)

Vault (4—Hidden assets)

To dream of a locked vault indicates someone is withholding from you something that is rightfully yours. This is for their own selfish gain. Make an investigation and see if you can discover what this dream is trying to tell you.

Vegetable (7—A good investment soon)

To dream of cooking, preparing, eating, or raising vegetables that grow above the earth indicates money made through commerce. To dream of vegetables that grow under the earth indicates money made through oil or mining.

Veil (3—You will take treatments for your hair)

To dream you wear a veil or see others wearing one indicates you should not let others lead you into something you do not want to do.

Velvet (See Silk)

Vine, Vineyard (See Grapes)

Violet (See Flowers)

Visit (7—A spiritual visit indicated)

When you dream of visiting with a person, your spirit actually does make contact with that person while you sleep.

Volcano (1—Beware of a fight)

To dream of a volcano indicates a stormy argument.

Vulgar (9—Change some of your friends)

To dream you see or hear vulgarity indicates someone will conduct themselves in such a way as to make you unhappy in their company. This is not a good dream.

> *That holy dream—that holy dream,*
> *While all the world were chiding,*
> *Hath cheered me as a lovely beam*
> *A lonely spirit guiding.*

Edgar Allan Poe

▼ W ▼

Wages (See Money)

Wait (8—Go forward and win)

To dream you are waiting for someone or someone is waiting for you indicates you are wasting time. You are not making the most of your opportunities. Don't put off until tomorrow what you can do today.

Walking (5—A good dream)

To dream you are walking indicates health, strength, and success.

Wall (3—A change for the better)

To dream of a wall indicates obstacles. To climb over a wall indicates that these obstacles will be overcome. To dream of painting or papering the walls of your home indicates a change for the better coming into your home.

Want (4—Do not be slovenly)

To dream of poverty or that you are in poverty indicates that you should practice thrift and keep your affairs above board. This is a warning that it might actually happen to you.

War (6—Indicates war)

To dream of war indicates you will hear much wrangling between nations, which will worry you considerably.

Wart (8—Do not speak of an old disagreement)

To dream of warts indicates a small worry and that some money is coming your way.

Washing (9—A fresh start for you)

To dream of washing clothes and working hard at it indicates you will make a great change in your household, and you will clean out all the petty annoyances that bother you.

Watch (See Jewels)

Water (4—A good dream)

To dream of vast bodies of water, such as the ocean, a large lake, or a big river, on the whole is a very fine dream. To dream of swimming indicates that your affairs will run smoothly for some time to come. To dream of a ship docking indicates a pause before prosperity. To dream of an industry where water is used in vast quantities indicates prosperity. A dream of clear water in any form is a good dream. Muddy water indicates worry and trouble. To dream of many ships and boats on the water indicates vast fortunes.

Weather (8—A good dream)

To dream that the weather is mild and delightful indicates happiness and good health. Foggy weather indicates sadness. (See Rain)

Weaving (2—A new venture soon)

To dream of weaving indicates that you are laying a solid foundation for the future. Be patient and you will succeed. This is a good dream.

Wedding (3—A good dream)

To dream of attending a beautiful wedding indicates great happiness coming into your life. Trying on wedding clothes, whether you are married or single, is a very good dream. If single, it indicates a new sweetheart and a proposal. To dream of trying on a wedding ring, if single, indicates a marriage within a year. To dream of your own wedding ring indicates a promise to be paid. A beautiful wedding on the whole is a very fine dream.

Weed (1—Caution in business)

To dream of weeds in your garden indicates that people will try to put obstacles in your way so you will not succeed. To dream of destroying weeds means you will triumph over your enemies.

Weighing (See Scales)

Well (7—Good advice from a friend)

To dream of an old-fashioned well where you draw the water up in a bucket indicates great satisfaction in what you are doing, and you will see the day to show those who told you you would fail that you really have succeeded.

Wharf (See Water)

Wharf (3—You are longing for a trip)

To dream you are on a wharf and it is loaded with merchandise and big steamers are tied to the wharf indicates a long sea voyage. This may not take place at once, especially if the wharf is loaded with merchandise. The merchandise indicates that this is coming. To sail on a beautiful steamer from this wharf indicates new adventures and happiness in store for you. This is a very good dream.

Wheel (8—Do not bear the burden of others)

To dream of wheels indicates that you will spend much time in straightening out your tangled affairs.

Widow (2—You will start something alone; it will be good)

To dream of a widow or that you are a widow indicates sadness, loneliness, and a change for the better in your life.

Wife (7—A good dream)

To dream of your wife indicates that she loves you.

Wig (3—Study and read)

To dream of a wig indicates that someone is trying to hide knowledge from you.

Wild Animals (9—A good dream)

To dream of wild animals which are used for food is a good omen. It signifies plenty. To find them dead in the woods indicates waste and warns of coming loss.

Will (See Estate)

Wind (5—Hasty news on the radio)

To dream the wind is blowing gently means happiness. A strong gale means danger, trouble, and angry words. Be careful after you dream of a wind storm.

Window (7—Try and you will win)

To dream you look out of the window indicates a very small thing is keeping you from the success that is yours. Investigate.

Wine (6—A good dream)

To dream you drink wine indicates coming prosperity. In fact, to drink mildly of any wine or hard liquors means the same. To dream you become intoxicated means you lose opportunities through a lax condition or action on your part. Liquor of any kind represents prosperity. After you dream of liquor, conduct yourself and your affairs so you may profit from this dream.

Wire (1—You will see many animals soon)

To dream of wire indicates that you will have friendly support and cooperation in your work. This is a good dream, unless it is barbed wire, which warns you of danger.

Witness (1—A good dream)

To dream you are called upon to be a witness indicates that you will have to help your friends.

Wolf (See Animals)

Wood (3—New furniture)

To dream of cutting wood, a big wood yard, or any form of wood indicates that you should use your ideas and experiences of yesterday to succeed in the future. Wood is a very fine dream.

Work (4—Good days ahead)

To dream you have work to do indicates that you will have plenty to do. This is a good dream.

Worms (7—Money from the earth)

To dream of worms indicates that you will have work to do which is dirty and distasteful.

Worry (8—Sadness)

To dream you worry or grieve is an indication that you are not concentrating on what you really should do.

Wound (See Accident)

Wreck (See Accident)

Wrinkle (2—Not a good dream)

To dream you see someone else's or your own face wrinkled indicates that petty worries will assail you. It also indicates that worry can do more harm than a hard sick spell.

Write (3—You will be very busy)

To dream you are writing letters or anything else indicates that you will sign a note and care should be used as to what you put in writing.

> *And he said, "Hear now my words, if there be a Prophet among you, I the Lord will make myself known unto him in a vision, and will speak unto him in a dream."*

Numbers xii, 6

▾ Y ▾

Yacht (See Water)

Yardstick (See Measure)

Yarn (4—You will be invited to a luncheon)

To dream of yarn or that you are knitting indicates a warm friendship or a happy gathering. This is a good dream.

Yeast (7—Forge ahead)

To dream of yeast means you should beware of people's inflated ideas.

It also indicates that you will rise above your present station in life through your own efforts.

▾ Z ▾

Zipper (9—Ask questions; it will help you)

To dream of a zipper indicates that someone will keep from you something you really should know. After this dream, be a little inquisitive and investigate. It also indicates you should keep your own affairs to yourself.

Zodiac (3—A welcome change)

To dream of a zodiac indicates there will be a big change in your life before the year has passed.

Zoo (1—Loss through carelessness)

To dream of a zoo or a circus or anywhere animals are confined means you are not doing the things you should because you would rather enjoy yourself instead of working. This is an indication that you should stop chasing butterflies and settle down to good solid work; otherwise you may be confined due to a shortage of funds.

He whom a dream hath possessed knoweth no more of doubting.

Shaemas O'Sheel

Planetary Hour Guide

My Chinese teacher in the Orient taught me that planetary hours were very important in everyday life. To make them as simple as possible, so that anyone can understand and use them, I have given you here a brief Planetary Hour Guide.

The astrological day begins at the exact moment of local sunrise, and the night begins at local sunset. The time between sunrise and sunset is divided into twelve equal parts, each of which is called one planetary hour. Similarly the time from sunset to sunrise is also divided into twelve equal parts which constitute the planetary hours of the night.

The first planetary hour, starting from sunrise on any day, is ruled by the planet ruling the day itself. The succeeding hours are ruled by the planets in a definite and fixed succession, known as the Chaldean order, which is as follows: Saturn, Jupiter, Mars, Sun, Venus, Mercury, and Moon. Thus on a Sunday the first hour from sunrise is ruled by the Sun, the next hour is ruled by Venus, the next by Mercury, the next by the Moon, the next by Saturn, and so on in the same order throughout all the remaining hours of the day and night. It is a simple matter to work out the planetary hours for any give day once the time of sunrise and sunset have been taken from the almanac, but for those who need merely a close approximation, there are numerous mechanical devices on sale that give the commencing times of each hour for various latitudes and their planetary rulers at a glance. Therefore it is necessary to know the times of sunrise in your own locality, since that tells us when the planetary day begins. The time of sunrise depends on the longitude of any given place, and of course it varies with the seasons. Moreover, the *difference* in time at these various places does not change. Get your local time of sunrise each day as a starting point.

The planetary hour depends on the day of the week and the position of the sun during that day, and of course we know the position of the sun is never the same in the various time zones.

S U N R I S E

Sun	Mon	Tues	Wed	Thur	Fri	Sat
Sun	Moon	Mars	Mer	Jup	Ven	S'tn
Ven	S'tn	Sun	Moon	Mars	Mer	Jup
Mer	Jup	Ven	S'tn	Sun	Moon	Mars
Moon	Mars	Mer	Jup	Ven	S'tn	Sun
S'tn	Sun	Moon	Mars	Mer	Jup	Ven
Jup	Ven	S'tn	Sun	Moon	Mars	Mer

N O O N

Mars	Mer	Jup	Ven	S'tn	Sun	Moon
Sun	Moon	Mars	Mer	Jup	Ven	S'tn
Ven	S'tn	Sun	Moon	Mars	Mer	Jup
Mer	Jup	Ven	S'tn	Sun	Moon	Mars
Moon	Mars	Mer	Jup	Ven	S'tn	Sun
S'tn	Sun	Moon	Mars	Mer	Jup	Ven

S U N S E T

Jup	Ven	S'tn	Sun	Moon	Mars	Mer
Mars	Mer	Jup	Ven	S'tn	Sun	Moon
Sun	Moon	Mars	Mer	Jup	Ven	S'tn
Ven	S'tn	Sun	Moon	Mars	Mer	Jup
Mer	Jup	Ven	S'tn	Sun	Moon	Mars
Moon	Mars	Mer	Jup	Ven	S'tn	Sun

M I D N I G H T

S'tn	Sun	Moon	Mars	Mer	Jup	Ven
Jup	Ven	S'tn	Sun	Moon	Mars	Mer
Mars	Mer	Jup	Ven	S'tn	Sun	Moon
Sun	Moon	Mars	Mer	Jup	Ven	S'tn
Ver	S'tn	Sun	Moon	Mars	Mer	Jup
Mer	Jup	Ven	S'tn	Sun	Moon	Mars

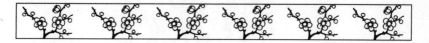

Sunday is ruled by the Sun

Monday is ruled by the Moon

Tuesday is ruled by Mars

Wednesday is ruled by Mercury

Thursday is ruled by Jupiter

Friday is ruled by Venus

Saturday is ruled by Saturn

In seeking to avail oneself of the planets, the chart below should be considered. These influences are affected by the relative position of the planets at any given time, but in general the following holds true:

Good	**Bad**	**Neutral**
Venus	Mars	Mercury
Moon	Uranus	Neptune
Sun		
Jupiter		

The Chinese Horoscope

The Chinese linear year is divided into twelve months of twenty-nine or thirty days. The calendar is adjusted to the length of the solar year by the addition of extra months at regular intervals.

The years are arranged in major cycles of sixty years. Each successive year is named after one of twelve animals. These twelve-year cycles are continuously repeated. The Chinese New Year is celebrated at the first new moon after the sun enters Aquarius—sometime between January 21 and February 19. (*Information Please Almanac, 1982*)

Rat	Ox	Tiger	Hare	Dragon	Snake
1888	1889	1890	1891	1892	1893
1900	1901	1902	1903	1904	1905
1912	1913	1914	1915	1916	1917
1924	1925	1926	1927	1928	1929
1936	1937	1938	1939	1940	1941
1948	1949	1950	1951	1952	1953
1960	1961	1962	1963	1964	1965
1972	1973	1974	1975	1976	1977
1984	1985	1986	1987	1988	1989
1996	1997	1998	1999	2000	2001

Horse	Ram	Monkey	Rooster	Dog	Boar
1894	1895	1896	1897	1898	1899
1906	1907	1908	1909	1910	1911
1918	1919	1920	1921	1922	1923
1930	1931	1932	1933	1934	1935
1942	1943	1944	1945	1946	1947
1954	1955	1956	1957	1958	1959
1966	1967	1968	1969	1970	1971
1978	1979	1980	1981	1982	1983
1990	1991	1992	1993	1994	1995
2002	2003	2004	2005	2006	2007

Each of the twelve annual signs of the Chinese zodiac has its own special attributes and characteristics.

Rat

In Chinese astrology, a most favorable sign. Rat people are generally both physically attractive and charming and have many acquaintances, though only a few close friends. They tend to be quiet, secretive, critical, and a bit self-centered. They are often late bloomers, coming into their own at age forty. Politics, government jobs, and business are good careers for Rat people to pursue. Rat people are highly emotional and lavish with their affection; they are likely to have many lovers. *Compatible signs: Monkey, Dragon, Rat.*

Ox

Outwardly patient and placid, the Ox, once crossed or angered, is unlikely to forgive or forget. Ox people are regular in their habits, and have a strong sense of direction. They are modest and understated in manner, but can be plagued by the need to be perfect in everything they do. Ox men and women are very devoted to home and family, and if you want a faithful partner you would do well to marry an Ox. They are generous and caring and believe that to give is better than to receive. *Compatible signs: Rooster, Snake, Ox.*

Tiger

Tigers are cautious—they distrust their first impressions and are slow in forming judgments. They are hard workers and their thirst for knowledge is immense; they tend to do well financially. Tiger people are well-liked and respected, but nevertheless, they often lack self-confidence. Tiger people are usually not very demonstrative with their affections, but young Tiger men and women tend to play romantic games. It is best for Tiger people to marry later in life when they will prove to be faithful mates. *Compatible signs: Dog, Horse, Tiger.*

Hare

Hare (or Rabbit) people do well in speculation or games of chance, but are often too conservative in nature to take advantage of this characteristic. Because they are objective, meticulous, and hold to traditional values, Hares are often attracted to careers as lawyers or diplomats. Hares can be show-offs, and crave luxury and the gratification of sensual appetites. Rabbits are slow to form relationships, but are tender and gentle and giving to loyal friends and mates. But watch out, spurn a Rabbit and love turns quickly to hate. *Compatible signs: Ram, Boar, Hare.*

Dragon

Dragons are not always what they seem. They can appear to have everything going for them, as love, success, and the respect of others come easily to them, yet they can be unhappy, insecure individuals. To compensate for feelings of inadequacy, Dragons can be bossy and opinionated. Dragon people possess leadership qualities and personal magnetism, but they are advised to use these talents with discretion lest they offend their friends. Their exacting standards can lead to disappointments in love. Dragons tend to promiscuity in youth, which can inhibit their ability to form lasting relationships. *Compatible signs: Monkey, Rat, Dragon.*

Snake

Snakes are glamorous and vivacious and seek to associate with others who enjoy the elegant life. While often sympathetic to those less fortunate, Snakes can be narrow-minded and stingy. They are smart and talented, but frequently reluctant to put their brains and talent to good use. Snakes can appear calm and content, but they are sensitive—easily hurt and deeply pained by rejection. They are very romantic and tend to be monogamous, but they can move quickly to a new love affair if the first one fails. *Compatible signs: Ox, Rooster, Snake.*

Horse

Those born in the year of the Horse are gregarious and fun-loving. They are generally very attractive and tend to be flamboyant in dress and manner. Horses are charismatic and popular, but can cause their loved ones grief, as they tend to prefer the social whirl to domestic life. They can be quick-tempered, impatient, and unsentimental; their cleverness and ability as public speakers make them good politicians. Horses are romantic, but fickle, and they are often more interested in the physical aspects of a relationship than in the emotional ones. *Compatible signs: Tiger, Dog, Horse.*

Ram

Sincere and sensible, Ram (or Goat) people are nature lovers, or very religious, and they work well with their hands. Ram people are often not very adventuresome; cherishing their creature comforts, they seek security and the good life. Rams tend to try for financially advantageous marriages, but when they fall deeply in love there are no strings attached—they do everything in their power to make the loved one happy. Ram people are passionate, frank, and fastidious. *Compatible signs: Boar, Hare, Ram.*

Monkey

Monkeys are talented and intelligent, and have a fine memory in addition to a lively sense of humor. While these people are gifted and often successful financially, their attention span is brief—if they cannot see immediate results they often abandon a project. Even though Monkey people can be shy, they do well in groups and social situations. Monkeys are trusting, romantic, and idealistic. They make devoted and faithful mates. *Compatible signs: Rat, Dragon, Monkey.*

Rooster

Rooster people are plucky, adventurous, and flamboyant. Blessed with intelligence, imagination, and artistic ability, they make sure that everyone knows it. Candid and outspoken, they can hurt feelings, even though their instincts are sound and their advice good. They make tender, considerate, and forgiving mates. *Compatible signs: Horse, Tiger, Rooster.*

Dog

People born in the year of the Dog make excellent friends. They keep confidences and are gracious and responsible. They are sensitive and can be quick to anger, but the anger never lasts and there is nothing malicious about them. Inwardly, Dog people are never quite sure of themselves and they tend to be pensive and fretful; therefore, they can be jealous and suspicious in romantic relationships, prone to imaginary anxieties. They need a lot of loving reassurances. *Compatible signs: Tiger, Horse, Dog.*

Boar

Boars possess all the most desirable traits of human nature—they are loving, trustworthy, loyal, gentle, and faithful. They are modest and unassuming, and so their excellent qualities may not be readily apparent on first acquaintance. They prefer a quiet life of comfort and financial security, and while shy, they can be quite lively with close friends. In romantic relationships they are very vulnerable and they become quite involved emotionally. *Compatible signs: Hare, Ram, Boar.*

Margarete Ward

October 16, 1890–October 17, 1977

In 1981, as *Gong Hee Fot Choy Tells Your Fortune* was republished in a new edition, bringing the total copies in print to 500,000, and as this expanded edition of the *Dream Book* was being planned, we interviewed her husband of forty-nine years, Edward Arnold Winfield.

The Publishers

Tell us about Margarete Ward's early years.

Margarete was a little over a year old when her mother and father died. I think it was during a flu epidemic in 1891. I almost died myself in the worldwide flu epidemic of 1918. She was raised by relatives— her stepfather's name was Ward, too, and I think he was her father's cousin. He and his wife had two children of their own. Margarete always considered them her half-brother and half-sister. Her stepfather worked for the railroad, he was the boss of the gang that worked on the railroad. He would work one place along the tracks for six months or so and then move on, so the family lived all over when Margarete was growing up. She lived in Ohio, in Kansas, in Cheyenne, Laramie, Salt Lake, Albuquerque, Needles. She lived in Denver, too; as close as I can figure she was ten years old then. She went to school there for a year or two with the nuns. They do a very good job of teaching, you know, and they helped her a lot. But, on account of all the moving, her schooling was broken up. She had very little formal education, though I think her stepfather did try to teach

her a little. Her stepmother just sort of cracked the whip on her all the time and Margarete had a lot of hard work to do when she was a little girl.

When did she leave home?

They were in San Bernardino when she came of age. She was sixteen or eighteen and she got away from the family. The movie business was just starting up. She met Mac Sennett, Ruth Roland, and Pearl White, who played in all those old serials that leave you in a state of suspense so you'll come and see the next one. She could have worked there if she wanted to, but she didn't go for that. She didn't like the movies; she might have been famous if she had.

So what did she do instead?

She went into partnership with another woman, modeling and selling dresses. I don't think she did any of the sewing, but she helped with the design of the dresses. She was in that business until World War I was over and then she went to China, to Shanghai. She'd always wanted to go to China and when she talked about it as a child, her stepmother used to get mad and slap her down. Her stepmother thought it was fool's talk.

She was in Shanghai until about 1925, as far as I can figure, working for selling and importing companies and sailing back and forth across the Pacific.

Did she speak Chinese?

No. She learned a few words and evidently she could speak enough to get along. Most of the business people she dealt with spoke English, so she didn't really need to speak Chinese. The people she met and did business with in China liked her real well, and she liked it over there from the way she talked about it.

What did she do when she came back in 1925?

She went back to Los Angeles. She met Charlie Chaplin then, and Sid Grauman, the man who built all those theaters around LA. She was the one who talked him into building the Chinese Theater. She worked for him when he designed and built it and he paid her for helping with it.

When did you meet her?

We met in 1928 at the Ambassador Hotel. We met accidentally. She had been living with some relatives, but when we met she had her own apartment on Oxford Street, and she had a police dog. It wasn't long after we met that we went to Reno and got married on April 23, 1928. She was 37 then. I'd just about given up the idea of getting married, but with her it was quite different. We had similar tastes and there was very little conflict.

Did she keep working after you were married?

Well, she had just written a story for Charlie Chaplin and was kind of freelancing that way. She was also working in real estate—she was in Texas on a real estate deal just before I met her. She was really an active woman.

After we were married, she was tired of traveling; she had already seen the world and she was ready to settle down.

Did she start writing then?

She had started to work on *Born to the Purple* before we were married, and in the early '30s she decided to put her fortune-telling game (*Gong Hee Fot Choy Tells Your Fortune*) together. She wanted to do something that would be an accomplishment. I said go ahead and see if you can get someone to print it. She got a company in L.A. to print the book and we put up all the money. I remember telling her that we were putting hard-earned money into this (it was the Depression then, remember) and I wanted to proofread it myself. I wanted to make it perfect, but she said no. She said it was good enough and so we went from there. It was first published in 1932 or 1933. I told her she was not charging enough for the book. The cost was $1, and the deluxe edition was $3.

How was Gong Hee Fot Choy received?

Oh, it was successful; it sold right off the bat. It was so successful that someone tried to copy it and went to the same printer. The other people never got anywhere with the game, but it caused some trouble between Margarete and the printer.

When the first printer died, Margarete started filling orders herself. We'd take them down to the post office. Then a company in Chicago took it over for a year or two, before we started printing it in Reno. That's when I started to figure out how many different arrangements of cards on the board were possible, how may different fortunes there could be. The printer and I worked out the number and took it to many, many places. I found a book on algebra and it proved that we had done it right.

When did she write the Dream Book?

She did the Dream Book right after the fortune-telling game. And then she published *Born to the Purple*, the book she was working on before we met. I still haven't read the book through. She wrote poetry, too. She planned on getting some of her poetry together for a book, but her health was failing and she couldn't work like she used to. She would read her poetry to me as she wrote it and I helped her with it sometimes. I thought I would complete and correct and publish her poetry someday.

Did a lot of people want to talk to Margarete about her psychic ability?

Yes, but it was a real drain on her. In LA. they would say you were doing it for the money, and she didn't like that. She wanted to print her book on prophecy, but she was held back by the printer. I told her to be more forceful, but the printer didn't want to do it. But she knew the truth about things, she knew it all right.

Did Margarete feel success in her life?

Yes, she felt a certain amount of success. She finished her book and her game, but she had visions of doing more. People always wanted her to demonstrate her *Gong Hee Fot Choy* and she did a lot of that in department stores. She got a lot of fan mail which she always tried to answer. And a man in San Francisco wrote a song for her called "Margie."

What did she do for pleasure?

We used to make pleasure trips out of our business trips. She didn't like night clubs or that stuff. We didn't go to the movies much, but after 1948 they started showing them on television a lot, so we watched television for pleasure. And she really liked her dogs.

Didn't she believe in reincarnation?

Yes, we both did. But she didn't like death at all. She would never go to any funerals, she always sent me. She thought she was going to die a lot of times. She was sick in the 1930s and then she got stronger. At the last she had arteriosclerosis and she had had several strokes. When she was younger death was horrifying, but when death came to her she was not afraid, because she had faith in what was after death. She stood up to death perfectly. She was a very happy person.

A Dream

By Margarete Ward

Some time during the night
My soul wandered away
To a far distant land
Where I lived another day

I was driving my car
As in days long ago
Going to a tiffin
In a cave far below

The streets were so narrow
I parked on a ledge
I had to pass over
A rustic old bridge

I stopped there to gather
Some lotus flowers rare,
And watch the golden fish
A swimming here and there

Many trees were holding
This old swinging bridge
I tripped over lightly
Far away from the edge

My arms full of flowers
In this cool shady spot,
I hated leaving there,
The tropic sun, was so hot!

My friends were now waiting,
And a good tiffin too;
Time flies, I had to go
Nothing else I could do

So I promised myself
I would return another day
To walk over this bridge
And watch the fishes play

Just then I awakened
By the mocking bird's call
I found it was morning
And a dream after all.

Dream Log

_____
_____
_____
_____
_____
_____
_____
_____
_____
_____
_____
_____
_____
_____
_____
_____
_____
_____
_____
_____
_____
_____

Dream Log

Dream Log

Dream Log

_____
_____
_____
_____
_____
_____
_____
_____
_____
_____
_____
_____
_____
_____
_____
_____
_____
_____
_____
_____
_____
_____